DEATH
of the
GOOD GIRL

*A Memoir of Love,
Betrayal, and Courage*

DR. TERESA TAYLOR WILLIAMS

TRAITMARKER MEDIA

DEATH
of the
GOOD GIRL

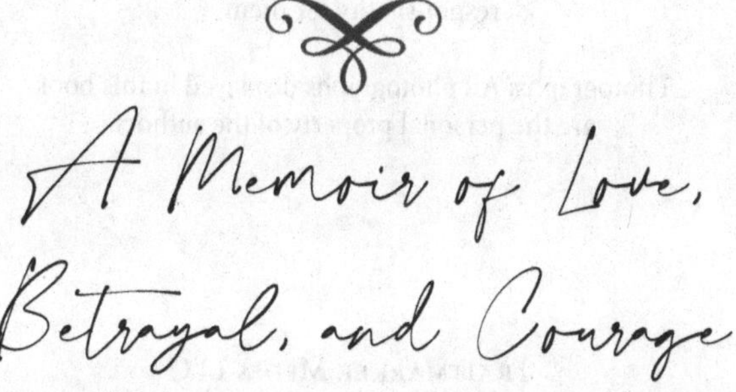

*A Memoir of Love,
Betrayal, and Courage*

DR. TERESA TAYLOR WILLIAMS

Traitmarker Media LLC
www.traitmarkermedia.com
traitmarker@gmail.com
Editor: Sharilyn S. Grayson
Cover Design: Robbie Grayson III

PUBLICATION DATA

1) BIOGRAPHY & AUTOBIOGRAPHY—
Cultural, Ethnic & Regional / African -American & Black
2) FAMILY & RELATIONSHIPS—Death, Grief & Bereavement
3) BUSINESS & ECONOMICS—Women & Business

Paperback: 979-8-8690-0071-2

A Note from the Publisher

The publisher and the author are providing this book and its contents on an "as is" basis and make no representations or warranties of any kind with respect to this book or its contents and disclaim all such representations and warranties, including but not limited to warranties of mental healthcare for a particular purpose.

The content of this book is for informational purposes only and is not intended to diagnose, treat, cure, or prevent any mental condition or disease. This book is not intended as a substitute for consultation with a licensed practitioner. Please consult with a physician or healthcare specialist regarding the suggestions and recommendations made in this book.

Contents

PART II | *The Strong Woman*

Good Girls Should Die

Can silence kill? I feel it could. I'm writing my story today because I realize that silence would surely kill me. Repressing the painful memories inside me will destroy me. The bitterness and anger not purged from my system will continue to prevent a healthy future.

I'm a mother, teacher, advisor, friend, daughter, and aunt, but the role I was trained to fill from the age of nine—and the one that made my life complete—was being a wife. There was no greater feeling of contentment and security than to feel engulfed in the arms of my man. Just as Tony Award-winning singer Heather Headley sang in her song "He Is," my husband was to me the protector, the lover, the friend, the comforter, and the provider. Interestingly, other than referring to a lover, these roles also can be ascribed to God.

Did I worship my husband as I did God? No. But I did respect and love him, just as he did me. I believed him and in him. Was he good to me? Yes! And I was good to him. My husband opened my eyes to many things and helped me see a world I had no idea even existed. We danced the night away at clubs, enjoyed edgy off-Broadway theater, and shopped at the exclusive Bergdorf Goodman. He rescued me from the little cave where I lived, growing up as a little mixed-race girl on 200th Street in Queens, New York.

In my early years, I felt that my home and neighborhood were heavenly. My mother and I would take walks around the beautiful blocks where I loved to skip and feel the breeze on my face. By the time I entered elementary school, my neighborhood changed. In my pre-adolescent years, the beauty and serenity of our walks disappeared and were replaced with isolation and fear. My mother and grandmother sternly warned me to stay inside and never leave the stoop.

My neighborhood was no longer heavenly. It was a war zone of drugs and crime, and my family's answer was to keep me locked inside the house. Seclusion and sadness overwhelmed me, and I no longer skipped my way anywhere. Can you imagine a life so solemn that you couldn't imagine growing up to be thirty? *I* couldn't imagine growing up. Why?

Among the many reasons was seeing firsthand the realities of Black ghetto life. What had once been a beautiful block lined with bright tulips, tall trees that seemed to touch the sky, trimmed lawns, clean streets, neatly painted houses with well-kept cars in the driveways, and carefree children sitting on the stoops or playing ball turned into a nightmare war zone filled with neglected homes, gunfire, and the invasion of the drug trade with its crack pipes, dirty needles, and gangs that constantly battled for territory.

During this time in my life, I lived in a sort of bubble created by my family. The one thing I still enjoyed was my mother reading to me. Some nights, she read me fairy tales from my set of Hans Christian Andersen with stories like "The Little Mermaid" ("The Little Sea-Maid") and The Brothers Grimm fairy tales with stories like "Hansel and Gretel." But of all fairy tales, the story I loved the most was "The Teeny Tiny Woman."

It became an obsession of mine to have my mother read me this very short story. The story told of a teeny tiny woman who lived in a teeny tiny house with teeny tiny children and a teeny tiny spouse. The story helped me envision being so teeny tiny that I could almost not be seen. I could be so tiny that nothing bad could happen to me. Listening to my mother read, I could believe that even though the world as I had known it was crumbling, being teeny tiny and almost invisible through remaining obedient, silent, and good would help me disappear and be safe.

Ironically, my husband nicknamed me Tiny. He said that when he first met me, though I was almost six feet tall and looked like a model, I always seemed to want to shrink, to hide, and to disappear. He was right. Many times in my life I have wanted to be teeny tiny so that the world couldn't hurt me and others couldn't see me.

Through a series of soul-shaking surprises, unbearable heartache, life-and-death decisions, and the threat of losing everything, I learned not to be so tiny anymore.

I learned to be strong.

Part I
The Good Girl

Drowning

I had to kill. It was the only solution for my survival. Living under siege, enemies infiltrated my heart and my home. Conspiracy surrounded me and closed in with the help of my man. I killed the "Good Girl." If I hadn't, I would have surely died.

My fear? Drowning.

I've heard that drowning is one of the most painful of deaths. The water seeps down slowly, filling your lungs as they tighten hard. You stay conscious long enough to know what's happening, but you cannot help yourself. It's like paralysis has set in, and you are watching without the ability to speak, fight, or move.

It's like you're in a pool, holding onto the sides because you can't swim. But you edge along, and then someone pushes you into the deep end where your feet find no ground. Your head will surely go under, and you will flail around wildly and desperately, trying to grab onto something stable. But nothing—no one is there. You are going down but you don't want to believe or admit to it.

This is the slow, torturous death you never imagined until a side chick found her way into your home, and every breath you take is strangling the little bit of air, fight, and consciousness you can summon because she's taken your life raft, too. And where he would have jumped in to save you, he's now numb to your impending doom.

1

A Heritage of Strength

I was a good girl. I always obeyed my parents and grandparents and aunts and uncles, and any adult, come to think of it. I never talked back and always followed the rules.

In my childhood home, we children had our place, and we stayed in that place. Adults had their roles, and we never questioned their decisions, choices, or actions. To do so was to invite a look, a pinch, or a stare that would bring a cold shiver reverberating through your bones, tears running down your cheeks, or pee trickling down your leg. Everything was divided into "for grown folk" and "for kids," and the two never intertwined.

This way of life tied into the concept of respect—the same respect I observed between my elders, who never argued with each other, at least not in front of others and especially not in front of me. I equated respect with treating another person as a leader. Someone to admire and trust.

Though the women in my family deferred to their husbands, they were not weak, docile, or fearful. They simply tempered their respect, dressed it up, and served it to their mates on a silver platter. Not on a garbage can lid.

Through my eyes, what it meant for my great-grandfather, grandfather, and father to be treated like kings was that they got respect. I can recall hearing my grandmother asking my grandfather what he thought about an issue. She would respond with, "You're so right," or "I thought so," or "You always have the answer." The funny thing was that I would also hear her on the phone saying to a close friend, "I'm making up my own mind. I thought about what he said, but I'm going with my decision."

Growing up in a household of three generations of Black women, I saw that the respect and attention that the men in my house received was not too far removed from worship. While the men were undoubtedly the kings of the castle, the women knew that they were the queens.

My family was full of intelligent, diligent, and gifted people who were stifled by racism, discrimination, and lack of opportunity. My great-grandfather, who retired as a Red Cap for the railroad, woke up at 1 a.m. each morning to go to work. He was a tall, slender, retired serviceman who never left the house without his fedora, spit-shined wingtips, and suit. In fact, I don't ever recall seeing him without a suit.

My great-grandmother was a housekeeper for a highly decorated Army colonel, and she learned the rules of etiquette by keeping his house.

My grandfather retired from the utility company Con Edison. He worked underground where he carted the inspectors back and forth, waking up every day at 3 a.m. to catch the bus at 4 a.m. He never wore anything less formal than a white, short-sleeved, buttoned-down shirt and tie with his pressed slacks. And he always wore suspenders. He would don a suit jacket on Sundays for church.

My grandmother won Amateur Night at the Apollo as a singer and dancer, and she traveled on the road with the Nicholas Brothers, Lena Horne, Cab Calloway, and others. She made short films and was known as the "Sepia Kate Smith" who was known for singing "God Bless America."

But my grandmother also told stories of having to sleep in cars because hotels wouldn't accept Black performers as guests. She also remembered concert venues where she had to enter through the back door. The front door was closed to "niggers." While White audiences could enjoy being entertained by my grandmother and her peers, they couldn't walk through the same door.

My father worked at the military hospital and wore a starched uniform. He got off work around 2 a.m. In later years, he owned a car service and changed his uniform to a buttoned-down shirt paired with perfectly ironed slacks as his daily wear. Every one of these men wore a watch. According to my grandmother, a watch was a sign of a working man. She'd say, "A man without a watch is a man without responsibility. But a man with a watch? He has places to go, places to be on time."

My mother was brilliant. She was the only Black girl in her graduating class from high school. Bell Laboratories selected her to work for them after graduation, which today would be like being selected to work for Apple. My mother taught me many things, and I embraced much of her advice. The quality I most appreciated about her was her tenacity—never stop fighting for what you are entitled to receive until you have won.

Our household stood out in other ways as well. We were not a loud house by any means.

I was born into an interracial neighborhood and a multi-ethnic household. I was not uncomfortable being around White people. My grandfather, my uncles, and my aunts were all of mixed race, as was my mother. Their heritage was visibly obvious to others. My mother and her sisters had beautiful, long, thick, flowing hair. I remember the day my mother and her sisters came around the corner from the hair salon, smelling of sweet hair spray and sporting a new hairstyle called the "beehive."

Growing up on my block in St. Albans, New York, in a two-family house with a livable attic, I observed how the women of the block, dressed in aprons and cotton, collared dresses, kissed their husbands at the door. When the men pulled off in their cars, the wives would quickly run out with broom in hand and sweep the walk. Later, they would pull weeds from the front lawn. Around 3:30 p.m., their day outside seemed to end as they stopped the group chats and went inside to prepare dinner.

We were middle class. My mother and her sisters wore tailored dresses, high heels, nylons, and pearl necklaces, and they carried white gloves to work and church. Their makeup was always done to perfection. They were my perfect images of women.

Despite my benefiting from this heritage of strong, respectful people, I was sad as a little girl. A large part of my sadness came from growing up in a transitioning neighborhood. While I was mixed race, I was cultured. On the one hand, I was constantly ridiculed by my darker-skinned, curlier-coiffed classmates. On the other hand, I was rejected by the White students. I wore starched school dresses with white Peter Pan collars, lace-trimmed anklets, and black patent leather shoes. My crinoline slip extended my pleated skirt.

Had I attended a preparatory school, my style

would have worked. But I lived in an area that was rapidly deteriorating because of White flight and the overpopulation of single-family homes that were stretched to accommodate several generations of tenement dwellers from the outer boroughs.

In the midst of a bad place, I was a good girl. And I learned the lessons of life from my bedroom window as the violent gang war for drug territory played out right by my front stoop. Before the change in my neighborhood, I could sit on the stoop on Sundays when the block was quiet, and I would watch the cars go by on the boulevard. My neatly kept block of one-family and two-family homes was beautiful, with lush trees, green lawns, bright tulips in the spring, and sprinklers in the summer. After the neighborhood changed past repair, I witnessed a murder out my front window by that same stoop one summer night.

Three generations of strong women saved me from the crack, alcohol, and prostitution of my neighborhood by watching me constantly, keeping me under lock and key, and never allowing me to go out and play with the new kids on the block. So, in middle school, I didn't smoke weed, shoot crack, or snort coke as my neighbors' kids were doing excessively. I was a loner.

Needless to say, growing up in a household where rules were firm and never bent produced a scared little girl who felt afraid of everything outside home while she simultaneously had to navigate the world.

Anytime I sought to venture into uncharted waters, the authoritarian voice of one of three women—or all of them at the same time—stopped me. There was very little time, if any, that I was left alone to do for myself.

From the age of nine, I was under the tutelage of these three women. They taught me to live a life that was right. In that life, you did your chores, went to work (which was school for me), and kept your house clean. *Super* clean. *Neurotically* clean. I cleaned every day. I was raised to be a wife, after all.

The women in my family worked hard, scrubbing floors on their hands and knees, doing other people's laundry, and keeping other people's children. But their primary role was to be good wives and mothers. So, the work they did for others paled in comparison to the work they did at home for their own husbands and families. Seeing what a good girl I became under their influence, how could I have escaped this destiny that surrounded me until the day I, too, married?

2

The Making of the Good Girl

My family was like the family in the 1961 movie *A Raisin in the Sun,* starring Sidney Poitier. My mother and father wanted to move up in the world. They worked hard to save for a home in Queens and leave their newlywed apartment. Because my mother worked every day, my caretakers from birth were my grandmother and grandfather. My grandparents lived in Astoria, and the trip from my home in East Elmhurst to my grandparents' house added too much extra travel time to my parents' commute. As a result, I lived with my grandparents during weekdays from the time that I was a newborn. My great-grandparents helped care for me as well.

By the time I was six months old, my parents bought a home in St. Albans in a White, middle-class neighborhood of neat homes and groomed lawns. I don't recall hearing stories of racist threats or intimidation towards my family. Living among Whites was not new for us because our old neighborhood, Astoria, was mostly Italian with a sprinkling of other races.

My family home was divided into three stories. My great-grandfather and great-grandmother had the attic apartment. It was adorned with porcelain teacups, a settee, and silk curtains.

My grandparents lived on the second floor. My grandmother furnished her apartment in the same way that her Italian neighbors had. The curtains were bright and starched, and the living room windows were layered with silk, frilly tiebacks, and floor-length drapes. There was a hassock for your feet and porcelain figurines on the shelves.

The first floor was where my father, mother, brother, sister, and I lived.

I was an only child until I was six years old. During that time, I had the full attention of my grandparents and great-grandparents. Because I was the center of attention for those six years, I had the freedom to roam between floors and visit whenever I wanted.

I loved my grandparents with all my heart. I never gave them the choice of whether or not to have me visit—I simply loved being with them. Once I learned to use the key to open the door leading to the second floor, I would just appear. Sometimes, I would head upstairs at 7 a.m. They never turned me away.

My grandmother's answer to everything was to "take it to the Lord." As soon as I was able to read, she gave me a magazine that came in the mail every month called *Wee Wisdom*. It had pages to color, Bible stories, and a shiny, colorful cover. I loved it!

My own household, however, was unsettling to me. My parents worked long hours, which made them frazzled and occasionally short on patience. My source of comfort, fun, and attention was up that flight of stairs. My grandparents were my safe haven. I would wake up every Saturday morning, dress myself, and head upstairs to hot biscuits, coffee, and bakery buns. Being with them was the absolute best part of my life.

My mother's sister also moved to the new house. She was young and single, and she worked at a high-end store in Manhattan called Arnold Constable. My mother's oldest sister was an administrator at Gertz department store.

Between my aunts and my mother, I was dressed like a child model. I wore starched dresses with white collars and petticoats, anklets with lace trim, patent leather shoes, princess collars, and designer coats. I carried a muff in the winter to keep my hands warm.

I ate at restaurants in Manhattan, went to Radio City Music Hall regularly, and sat in the bleachers for the Macy's Thanksgiving Day Parade.

I was a dancer who studied ballet and tap at the Ruthie Barnes School of Dance on Jamaica Avenue. I had my hair done each week: pressed, curled, and styled. My room was decorated in taffeta drapes and matching spreads. I loved it! Who wouldn't? Among my other beloved rituals were acting in Christmas plays and attending Girl Scout church parades in which I carried the flag as a decorated Girl Scout.

I was safe when I was at home with my extended family. There, I felt that the world was perfect. I loved Saturdays because everyone was home. Besides being house cleaning day, it was the day when my mother and I would go to Green Acres Mall and shop. Saturday mornings were also my training day in the kitchen. I was happy on Saturdays.

Rising early, I would put on my housedress and do my hair in a bun. I would sit with my grandmother, learn to plan meals, and make meatballs and sauce from scratch the way that her Italian neighbors had taught her. I learned to chop and fry onions and combine the perfect ingredients to make the spaghetti sauce that cooked for hours for Sunday dinner. Why traditionally made Italian spaghetti sauce? We were "Black Italians" by way of Astoria, New York, our first home in Queens.

No one could get shirts whiter or starched stiffer than my grandmother. She would mix white chunks of starch and water in a big basin and lay each shirt in this concoction until fully saturated. After that, the shirt was pulled from the sink, wound up like a rope, twisted, and tied tight. It was left like that for a day. On the next day, the starch was rinsed out and hung on the line to dry. On the third day, it was ready to be steam ironed. I challenge anyone to beat my grandmother's shirt-starching method.

I spent my summer vacations from school in intensive home classes. I learned how to hang clothes on the line without falling out of the window. We never had mops in my house. I scrubbed floors with huge brushes on my hands and knees and waxed them with a giant towel.

I washed windows and blinds on the first and second floors. These were the days before plastic or wood and the metal blinds cut your fingers like knives. I was taught how to fill the tub with pine and ammonia mixed with the hottest water I could stand—so hot that rubber gloves served no purpose. I would put the blinds in to soak while I took out the screen and storm window for what seemed like fifty windows on a three-story house. I would shine the panes, each one separately, with paper towels. I would wash the sills and dig the bugs out of the cracks on the outside of the house. Today, no one would have tried these chores without a scaffold and belt. I can't count the times I nearly rolled down the slanted roof while the "new" kids laughed at me.

I loved the fact that I was brought up in a

three-generational home. I cherished coming home from the hell of school and sitting with my grandmother and grandfather at the kitchen table while my grandfather taught me to play pinochle and my grandmother taught me to cook. My world was safe and secure when I got back home. Saturdays were happy because I didn't have to leave the happy place that was home for the horrible place that was school.

I hated school.

I didn't feel safe as a child because I was the victim of bullying from everyone at school, including my teachers. I didn't fit in, and I didn't belong. A feeling of not belonging permeated most, if not all, of my life because of my differences. I can relate to the kid who is too tall, too pudgy, considered an "old soul," or who doesn't conform to a racial stereotype. I hated leaving my home, where life was kind and loving, and going to a place that only offered terror.

My grandfather walked me to school every day. From nursery school through second grade, "Papa" and I would hold hands as we walked. When I entered P.S. 136 Queens, the first thing I noticed was the wet and moldy smell of leaky bathroom pipes and nasty cafeteria soup. The building was also dark. The bathrooms were dirty, and the teachers were mean and scary.

What I will never forget was the way the other kids looked at me and treated me. In kindergarten, I sat at the head of a long table between two boys, one White and one Black. Every day, the White boy smelled like tuna, and the Black boy smelled like milk. The smells made me gag. These boys, along with the girls around the table, teased me about my dresses and party shoes. Most of all, they teased me about my skin color. These kids immediately hated me for my differences, calling me "strange" and "weirdo" and everything in between.

At first, I didn't understand that I looked any different from other Black children. At P.S.136, however, I learned new things about myself. As a little girl, I was round-faced, straight-haired, brownish-pink, pudgy, and mixed-raced. I had high cheekbones, rosy cheeks, and freckles. My hair was parted down the middle and braided in two long, thick braids. My skin was moisturized with lotion and Vaseline.

The other children taught me how to see myself through their teasing. I was teased the most about my face. As a group, the other children called me a "fat Puerto Rican Indian with a dirty face." But my face wasn't dirty. It was freckled. I just didn't realize it. Well into adulthood, I thought that my freckles were acne and felt ashamed.

Even as an adult woman, I recall two women, both Black and very Afrocentric, who volunteered their opinions that I was "strange." I now wonder if looking more like my Black classmates would have stopped the bullying and criticisms. I don't know. In my youth, the great divide in our community was all about the hair. Without that debate, would others have been my friends?

I grew up in a tough and cruel world that ostracized me. It was a lonely place to be isolated because of your individuality and differences. It was also frightening to think that no one would ever really understand and accept me other than my grandmother.

I was not the only Black girl in my classes. Still, I didn't connect with the other Black girls in school for the most part. Beyond color, we were just different. We had different experiences, even at that young of an age. However, our differences were not surprising, and they were not a newly discovered phenomenon. Explain it as you will, I didn't fit in. So, I suffered bullying in some form from the time I began elementary school until the time I graduated high school, though the word "bullying" was never used. It hadn't yet been invented.

By second grade, the adults in my life had determined that I had a problem because I spent part of every day in the nurse's office. She became my friend. Being in the classroom for endless hours and suffering through the isolation, bullying, and teasing had begun to take a serious toll on me. I cried every day. I developed stomach problems. I didn't eat. I kept to myself. I didn't interact with anyone. I just wanted to get to my safe place, the nurse's office, as soon as possible each day.

I remember a boy in second grade named Larry. He was short and mean. He fought with everyone. Rather, he beat up everyone. Friday after school was the time for all fights or "getting jumped." The event that turned the tide for me was the Friday that Larry decided to beat me up. I was walking to the corner of the block to cross the street away from the school. A crowd of kids followed me. Eventually, someone yanked my ponytail hard enough to jerk my head back. I turned around and saw Larry standing in front of me. The other kids pushed me into him, and the beating began. He said nothing to me. He just started pummeling me.

I can still recall my breath being taken from me when he punched me in the stomach. I tried to fight back but was unequipped. So I ran. The crowd followed, and Larry did, too. They tried to provoke me to fight, randomly screaming, "Fight! Fight!" and "Beat her!" Others shouted, "Think she's cute—acting like a White girl!"

I don't know how I got to my home, which was five blocks away, but the noise of the crowd was so loud that my grandmother looked out the window and saw me in the middle of this mob. The next thing I knew, my mother came flying out of the front door with a broom in hand, running towards me and swinging it. The kids ran away. But my problem wasn't over.

My mother, father, and grandmother knew that I had to return to school on Monday, so my mother went to school to confront the principal. Despite her intervention, I remember feeling depressed and frightened at the same time. I was scared to return to school and have a repeat beating from Larry or another boy. I hated my circumstances. To be among people who didn't like me and who had no semblance of ethical behavior, civil socialization, or respect for themselves or others was miserable.

Every Friday afternoon, I would walk around the block to Linden Boulevard to visit Miss Keys' Beauty Parlor. Miss Keys owned the beauty shop, and she had the front booth. The gap in her teeth only widened her smile when you entered the door. There were four booths, and Miss Russell, who did my hair, had the last booth. When you faced the wall in her booth, there was a window-sized cutout in the wall that gave a view of the kitchen. While doing my hair, she kept an eye out for the pot on the stove that contained the day's meal. Sometimes, it was collard greens or chicken. Other times, it was fish or pig feet.

The illegal numbers guy would come in every ten minutes, it seemed, to take bets from the women while Miss Russell pressed my hair. She would scoop out a dollop of blue grease and slap it on her wrist. When she pressed my hair, the smoke would billow from the iron like it was coming out of a chimney. Section by section, hot, long, thick hair, freshly pressed and curled, lay on my neck. Until I turned twelve, my mother walked me to the hair salon every week to see Miss Russell.

I was happy when the day came that I was allowed to go to the beauty salon on my own. I was so excited! The freedom and responsibility made me feel like a young woman on the path to womanhood.

My grandmother would hide the money for the hair salon somewhere on me. I would robotically walk to the salon and walk back. No detours. When my hair was all done, Miss Russell would call my house to let them know that she was sending me back around the corner. One day on this very route from getting my hair done by Miss Russell, my life changed.

Upon seeing my finished hair, I thanked Miss Russell as I routinely did and headed for the door. Before I could open the door, Miss Keys came running into the hair salon from outside, demanding that I stay where I was. I couldn't go out and walk home. Oblivious to what was happening outside, I stayed and waited as I was told.

My mother picked me up later that afternoon. I can still remember that day decades later. My mother firmly held my hand as we left the salon.

"Teresa, when I say close your eyes, you do it," my mother instructed me. "You understand?"

What? How could anyone give an order like that one to a curious twelve-year-old and expect her not to peek? But I was a good girl. I walked along with my mother, intending to obey.

At one point along the walk, she yelled to me, "Close your eyes!"

I immediately obeyed, but then, of course, I opened them. Even though there was a crowd, the corner was quiet. As my mother yanked me past the crowd, I noticed a light-skinned Black man with a black mustache and his hands folded across his chest. He looked richer than anyone I had ever seen. He didn't move. Dead.

I remember him so vividly. I can still recall the black derby he wore and the gray coat with its black velvet collar. If I close my eyes—as I should have done that day—I can see him now. His dead body haunted my memory and my imagination from then on. My life had changed forever. The neighborhood had changed forever, and things only got worse with every day.

So who was this man who was lying on my childhood corner, shot dead? The news quickly spread throughout my block. I also heard details not shared in my home when I returned to the hair salon the next week. The dead man had been a prominent drug lord who was trying to take over my neighborhood. He had been killed somewhere else, and his body was brought to the corner of 200th Street and laid there to make it clear to others who might have been thinking about infiltrating this neighborhood that it was off-limits. The danger of drugs and the devastation and change it would bring to our neighborhood would come quickly, and the consequences would affect everyone, including me.

No one in my house asked me how I felt about the dead drug dealer. My mother had told me to shut my eyes, and she assumed that I obeyed her. She didn't know that I had opened my eyes to peek. So when I started having anxiety, stomach issues, nervous tics like rocking back and forth, and a general fear of everything, my family simply thought me to be a sad child. But the memory of this man, a man who was once alive but had lain dead at my feet, haunted me.

The White families soon fled the neighborhood. No longer did tulips line the yards. No longer were houses neatly painted. With White flight came Black families from the inner city who would bring baggage with them. Though I would live at home for many more years, my childhood was effectively over.

3

Colored-in White Girl

When I think of my middle school and high school years, the words that come to mind are *tears, fear, anxiety, invisibility, confusion,* and *unhappiness.* My most vivid recollection happened one day in middle school when my teacher sent me to the guidance office to deliver an envelope during the period right after lunch.

The guidance office was at the end of a hall between the assistant principal's office and the nurse's office. I remember that the halls were strangely empty, and it was quiet. Beyond the nurse's office was an end stairwell. I ran down the stairs, heading towards the guidance office. At that moment, I saw liquid on the floor. As I got closer, I saw that it was red and that it ran from the stairwell into the hall.

It was the blood of a boy who was not a student at my school but who was one of the older kids who was always cutting school. Someone shot him in the schoolyard and dragged his body into the school. Now, there were no signs of the boy—just the blood left from his dead body.

I was fourteen. That gory sight was yet one more reminder that I was not safe—ever. In fact, if I summed up my school days with a phrase, it would be, "I was *never* safe."

Bullying followed me throughout my school years. Middle school brought the threat of worse fears than a Friday afternoon fight. It brought tough girls who enjoyed stomping you into the ground and even tougher teens who carried knives to scar your face.

I recall a middle school teacher, Mr. Lester, who didn't hide the fact that he didn't like me. He thought that I "upset the apple cart." Each year, he would re-hash years-old lesson plans and not expect ever to get questioned on the subject about things he didn't know. In his history class, I didn't have friends. Somehow, I was put with the students who were less enthused about school and who had no problem challenging or cussing the teacher out.

One day, Mr. Lester spoke to me about represent-ing the school at a conference in Albany, New York.

I was so honored and thrilled. He said that I was chosen because of my high grades and classroom performance. Little did I know that he was getting a big laugh out of sending me on this trip, because when the time came to leave, the bus was full of all the students that the faculty didn't want in school. While I thought that the trip was a reward for good work, the school used it as an opportunity to get rid of the unruly kids for the day.

The trip to Albany seemed endless. I was bullied the entire way there and back because one student called my coat a "dress." I had worn my best dress, thinking that representing my school was such an honor. My camel coat had a brown Peter Pan velvet collar and buttons. I still remember it to this day because it was one of my special coats.

The smirk on Mr. Lester's face the next day said it all. How evil was he? My school experience taught me that I couldn't even trust adult educators.

In ninth grade, I was inducted into the Arista Honor Society for academic excellence. Parents and local officials attended the candlelight ceremony. We wore black robes with white collars and yellow shawls and carried unlit candles down the aisle that we later lit as our names were called.

My entry into Arista was not so smooth. You had to have an average of 95% to be inducted. One teacher, Mrs. Sklar, was less than enthusiastic about students of color being inducted. The grade she marked on my last English paper put me at 94.7%, and she wouldn't change it.

Our typing teacher at the time, Ms. Miller, was a fierce woman and a fighter who was dedicated to education. Years later before she retired, she became principal of the school and then superintendent of the entire district. As the homeroom teacher for the Special Placement class for gifted students, she was very protective of her students. In many ways, she had to be because we were the target of bullies and non-supportive teachers. "Non-supportive" was putting it nicely. When Ms. Miller was unsuccessful in getting Mrs. Sklar to allow me to participate in the induction ceremony for Arista, she called my mother.

Enter the dragon.

Any phone call to my mother about school and me was a priority. It didn't matter what else my mother had to do, including going to her job—she was coming. And when I say that she was coming, you didn't want her to be coming for you.

Later, when I battled to get my own children through school, people said the same about me.

"You don't want her coming up to school for you!"

However, my mother was not a bully, and she didn't fight for anything I didn't deserve. She fought against mistreatment, discrimination, and racism for everyone. Her nickname was "Sister Sophie." When I got older, my nickname became "Mother Teresa." I'm proud to resemble my mother in this way. In situations of injustice, she was the mother to the world.

After an extremely early morning conference that included Ms. Miller, Mrs. Sklar, my mother, and the principal, Mr. Harris (a dark-skinned and broad former Army pilot), I was called down to the office to hear the verdict. Mrs. Sklar wore her usual scowl, and everyone else smiled. I found out that her decision had come down to the bibliography for my report. Mrs. Sklar took points off because my last two entries were not aligned with the margin. Ms. Miller told me that I had to reprint the bibliography and hand it in before the ceremony the next day. I did, and I marched.

While I never knew why Mrs. Sklar didn't like me, I think she didn't like any of the students of color in the gifted class. She always seemed to compliment the White children. Her attitude towards me was one of the many lessons I learned and stored away for later use.

In middle school, I had few friends. My best friend lived two doors down from my house. Her father was from India, and her mother was of mixed race. We were very close. I wished so badly that we had gone to school together. Her parents sent her to a Catholic school because they said that it was better. That decision left me alone.

Unfortunately, I was not lucky enough to be lifted out of the troubled school in my neighborhood. My path took me through many more years of bullying, torment, and fear in the cesspools of middle and high school. Feeling that you don't fit in is more than whether or not you get invited to parties or sit with the popular kids. It's about seeing others who are just like you.

Being alike doesn't have to do with skin color alone, but with others who see the world the way that you do. Experiences like the Albany trip and the Arista problem made me feel as if there was something seriously wrong with me.

Instead of learning to fit in with my peers, I learned to be a wife. Each Saturday, I pulled the shopping cart back and forth twelve blocks with a list a mile long. The shopping cart was my same height. Nevertheless, I got those groceries up two flights of stairs to my grandmother, who did all of the cooking. She made me watch her prepare and cook the meals so that "I could cook for my own" one day. My social time was going to church and singing in the choir. On Friday nights, a car horn would blow, and the pastor would pick me up along with the other teens to rehearse.

Am I strange? Is there something wrong with me? Why am I called a colored-in-white girl? These questions echoed inside me. I so wanted to fit in. I tried to get an Afro. I failed at that. My long, straight hair wouldn't transition into the curly hair needed to maintain an Afro. In fact, I cut my long hair regularly so that I wouldn't be told that I thought I was better than others.

I hated who I was. I hated myself because of how other people viewed me and treated me. Why would they treat me so badly if I were perfect like my grandmother believed? There had to be something wrong with me. Being around others never went well for me. Becoming a young woman intensified the differences between my peers and me.

During this time of rejection and loneliness, my grandmother was my everything. She comforted me, supported me, encouraged me, prayed for me, defended me, and listened to me. Most importantly, though, she understood me.

She seemed to be the only one who understood me. She understood me as an adult, and most importantly, she understood me when I was a child. I was always considered an odd child. I didn't speak much. I listened. I obeyed, and I learned. I was scared most of the time. I slept with my head completely under the covers at night. I slept in the front porch room, which had two walls of windows facing the street. In the summer, the windows were up, and I could easily hear the drunks, fights, and sirens. We didn't have a fence around our house, so anyone could walk up to my window and look into my room. Yes, there were blinds, but the hot summer breezes moved them. And behind the blinds lay a frightened little girl.

I was separated from my parents and siblings by the living room. In order to get to them, I had to run through the living room, down the hall, and past a side door, where stairs led down to the darkness of the basement.

I grew up with stomach aches all of the time. My doctor told my mother that I suffered from gastritis, which was a result of not eating breakfast. How could I swallow food in the morning with a nervous stomach? I ate when I was happy. I still do that today. The doctor suggested that I have cookies and milk by my bed every night so that I would eat it in the morning. Were cookies and milk magically going to make the children in my school look and dress like me? Were cookies and milk supposed to make school into a place where teachers were not mean or scary? Where there weren't fights every day at 3 p.m.? What were cookies and milk going to do for me?

No one ever listened to me describe the conditions I suffered except my grandmother, who was helpless to make anything better. What she did give me was her daily dose of faith through a tiny magazine called *Daily Word*. Since the age of fourteen, I have read *Daily Word* faithfully. I still do so today.

My grandfather—Papa—and I had also been close. He always smelled so good, and he wore a pressed white shirt with dress pants, suspenders, and a derby. Papa was a gentleman. His straight black hair was thick and shiny and combed back perfectly. You could see the freckles on his face through his fair skin. My Papa was German and Black. His mother was German, and his father was Black. At the time that they came together, interracial marriage wasn't legal. One day, his father, who was a seaman, left for an assignment. His boat was lost at sea.

One Sunday morning, I heard my grandmother's walking cane banging on the ceiling above. I sat straight up in bed and looked at my Sunday church dress that had been pressed and placed on a hanger. I heard the side door bang shut without being locked. My father flew out the door, and I heard his steps running hard up the stairs. My baby brother must have been in his crib. I never gave him a second thought.

Something was happening.

I ran out the side door and up the stairs to find my mother, father, grandmother, and great-grandmother in the living room. I couldn't see all the way in, but I didn't see Papa. My mother yanked me from the door of the living room and down the stairs to our floor and locked the door behind me.

Soon, I heard more footsteps going up the stairs. After what seemed like an eternity, my mother came into our house. I don't recall what she said to me. Her eyes were red. I couldn't hear her words. I didn't understand what was going on. The only image I have today is of a long, shiny, black car backing into the driveway while Black men in black raincoats were coming inside and up the stairs. It was silent. Just my mother and I stood in the driveway. My mother didn't say a word.

I heard the men coming down the stairs. When I saw them carrying a long, black plastic bag. I don't know why, but I instinctively started to run towards the bag. No one told me that my Papa was inside, but somehow I knew. I couldn't let him go. My mother grabbed my hand and pulled me back. I never saw my Papa again.

My grandmother, Katin (short for *Katherine,* my middle name), was everything to me—my life, and my breath, closer than my mother. The night my grandfather died, I took some things, threw them into a pillowcase, and moved upstairs to the second-floor apartment where she lived. I didn't leave her until I was twenty-four when I left for the church to get married.

I wasn't allowed at the funeral. I was considered too young. I felt as if something had been pulled out of my insides. I was anxious and confused, and as a result, I suffered from stomach aches and insomnia.

I didn't know why I couldn't say goodbye. My mother didn't understand. Papa was my protector, and I couldn't hold his hand or hug him again. Though I still had Katin, Papa's loss devastated me.

4

The Good Girl Held Captive

When I graduated from middle school, the close-knit group in Ms. Miller's homeroom class disintegrated as we went our separate ways. Many of my classmates in the IGC (intellectually gifted class) went to specialized high schools. I went to the neighborhood high school that was touted in a local newspaper in the mid-70s as having the "last White girl" in the school. It was one of the largest high schools in New York City. I lived close enough to walk.

Thug boys and tough girls ruled my high school. On Friday afternoons, school would end with a gang fight, if not more. For the girls, the weapon of choice was a flip-top from a soda can. One scrape across your face, and you were scarred for life. I don't know what the weapon of choice was for the boys, but from the evidence of shootings in the schoolyard, all guesses led to handguns.

How do you survive in a school building the size of a small town with multiple stairwells, entrances, and exits? How do you survive gangs within the building who claim the outer stairwells as their territory and then deal drugs and drink alcohol there? Smart students, or scared students, knew which stairwells to avoid.

Even the lunchroom was not a place where anyone could eat quietly with easygoing student chatter like you see on TV. The lunchroom in this building was in the basement, and the brutes who ruled our school came there not to eat but to pick on the smart students, to bully us, approach us for money, and make us their prey.

Among the student population were students who had special needs. Some had distinct facial structures. Many special education students also had physical handicaps, like a different gait in their walk or other physical deformities.

Due to so many problems with discipline, all students were forced to endure a captive lunch, which meant that no one could leave the building. You were trapped in this tomb with teachers who were oblivious to what we innocent students endured and who were probably just as intimidated by the troublemakers and scared of them as we were. Entering the cafeteria was like going into war without a gun. Gangs claimed tables and territory, and there was absolutely no real teacher supervision. With most of my friends gone to other schools and the few I had left from middle school having conflicting schedules, I was alone at lunch. So, as a matter of self-protection, I sat at the table with the special education students. They were nice, and the thugs mostly left them alone.

Early in the first month of school, a tall, athletic guy enrolled. Keith had the perfect Afro, a beautiful smile, and a goatee. He wore knit sweaters, fitted pants, and sneakers. He looked different from any of the other guys in my school. He looked older than the other boys in my class. On his first day of school, he was in a few of my classes. The band of wolves who called themselves schoolgirls gawked at him through the back doors of each class. I watched his reaction to these bruisers. He was unaffected.

At lunchtime on his first day of classes, I saw him come down to the cafeteria. He got a tray of food and sat alone. A few of those wolves passed by and attempted to throw their boobs and asses down his throat. Again, he seemed unaffected.

During the next day, he saw me in class and turned around to say, "Hi." I waved.

Lunchtime came, and I saw him come into the cafeteria. When he got his tray, he headed towards my table. He sat down next to me and started speaking to me very slowly. He chose his words carefully and spoke softly. He asked me how many regular classes I was allowed to take.

I responded, "Regular classes?" He said, "Yes."

It was obvious that he thought I was a special needs student because I was sitting near the table where the special needs students tended to congregate. I quickly cleared that misunderstanding up. I couldn't believe he thought I was in special needs! And I couldn't believe he was actually interested in me! After school, Keith protected me by leaving the school building to walk me safely to the bus since I had an early end of day and needed to get to work.

The next day, Keith walked me to my classes. By the middle of the day, I had to use the bathroom. So I took my life into my hands and entered the cloud of smoke inside the bathroom. Through the haze, I could see the ringleader of the girls' gang. Though I couldn't see her clearly, I heard her saying, "Don't come in here again, or you will regret it. If you come in here again, we will cut you." And one of her hench-girls threw a lit cigarette at me that just missed my hair. I immediately turned and ran out of the bathroom and never entered it again for the rest of high school. This encounter occurred in September of my senior year. For the rest of the year, I never went to the bathroom unless I was in gym. I still believe that this bullying is the reason for some of my bladder issues.

I hated the ridicule of girls who threatened me because my hair was too straight and long.

I looked like a wimp, and I was scared as hell of the bullying they practiced regularly. I was threatened with the knives that thug students brought into high school before there were metal detectors or searches. In those days, the bullying skanks would leave four tracks that stayed on your face for life by putting the flip tops on soda cans on each finger. Thank God, I was never a victim of the flips, but I did have lit matches thrown into my hair.

So, I ran home every day. The same girls who ripped faces up in fights with the flip-tops off soda cans hung out in a pit of promiscuity, violence, and drugs. I hated the life I lived, and I never enjoyed the parties others attended, the late nights in the park a few blocks away, or riding to the beach with the other kids on the block. My fellow students and their families, my new neighbors, had ruined my neighborhood.

As I said earlier, I saw murder in front of my house where the tulips lined the yard.

My father refused to give in to the new faction in the neighborhood. His house and yard remained neat and tidy. But the new neighbors didn't sweep or garden or maintain the yard the way he did. They threw their cigarette butts on the sidewalk, left beer cans on the stoop, screwed in the driveways or on the sides of the houses, and fought and cut each other when they drank too much.

The night of the murder I witnessed was a summer night. I was living on the second floor with my grandmother, where I had moved to be with her the night my grandfather died. My great-grandmother came running down the stairs. Alone. My great-grandfather had also passed years before. My father was asleep from long days of working his car service. My great-grandmother was screaming, "They're going to kill him! They're going to kill him." My grandmother and I ran to the front window. My mother called to tell us she was calling the police and to stay away from the windows and stay down.

But I had to see. There in front of my house in the middle of the street, at least fifty Black male teens had made a circle around one kid. They were standing on my mother's car and on neighbors' cars, cursing and throwing things. Some would punch and kick this kid. It was loud. The kid was begging for them to stop hurting him, begging for his life. My grandmother was screaming for me to get away from the window.

All of a sudden, one guy came out of the crowd. The crowd seemed to part ways for him. He reached into his pocket and pulled out a gun. I heard one scream from the crying, trembling kid. One shot to the head. Total silence.

Watching that senseless death was the first and only time I lost control of everything. I was shaking, crying, and wetting myself at once. I couldn't move. I still see the boy's body lying in front of my door.

And then they were all gone.

I wasn't allowed to watch the removal of the body. The blinds were closed.

Thankfully, I remained a prisoner for the four years of high school, locked in my home and not allowed to hang out with others on the block. It's the reason I'm here today.

What more can I say to describe high school? Here are some major highlights:

- Our class valedictorian got hooked on drugs and kicked out of Harvard.

- College advisement was restricted to the "upward-bound" students, of which I was not one. Therefore, I got no college advice.

- I was sent home with a common college application, and I put down Queens College because my father drove past there every day, heading to pick up fares with his taxi.

- Our senior prom was canceled because of too many drugs.

- Our senior trip was canceled. Students tried to flip the bus over and kicked out windows before we pulled off.

- My advisor said that I should take a commercial degree at a trade school.

- I graduated with a 94% average and didn't know what I had achieved until the ceremony when I was asked to stand.

- Neither math nor science was my best subject, and I worried about taking the Regents exam to graduate. Problem solved—someone broke into the school the night before and stole both tests.

I slipped through the cracks. Being quiet, shy, and attempting to be invisible actually worked for my good and my safety because I escaped the rough crowd. But being tiny also worked for the bad, as I received no college or scholarship opportunities.

5

Grandma's Little Girl

When I received my bachelor's degree in 1978, my job search took me back to my old middle school. My former principal and ninth-grade teacher were both still there. The school hired me and—ironically—I was now teaching alongside my former teachers.

I could walk to work every day through the same blocks where I had walked with my friends to school each morning as a student. Months into my job, I bought a car and drove this same path. But on rainy days before I bought my first car, my father, who owned a yellow medallion New York City taxicab, would drop me off at work.

One day, my father mentioned that after he dropped me off the previous day, he had made a fare. A man had flagged him down a few blocks from the school and paid for a drop to the same school where I was working. My father said that he had a good conversation with the man, who carried a big legal briefcase. The man told him that he was teaching while finishing law school. My father asked me if I had met anyone in the building that fit this description.

"No," I responded, "I hadn't."

Ironically, I eventually married this man.

The middle school where I worked served a neighborhood now made famous by then up-and-coming hip-hop icons. Today, the names Russell Simmons, Danny Simmons, Rev. Run, Jam Master Jam, Run DMC, and LL Cool J make that neighborhood the birthplace of artistic genius. But it took decades to repair the devastation of crack cocaine and gun violence that was prevalent both during my years as a student at the school and while I worked as a teacher in the same building.

Therefore, my father's question about whether or not I knew this teacher who carried a big legal briefcase—the teacher with big dreams—was one to which I could only answer, "No." I had survived the violence and drugs while I was attending the school by keeping my head down and minding my business. Now, I did the same as a teacher.

Many of my colleagues didn't like me. They felt I was the principal's and vice principal's pet because they knew my story of being a former student who did well out of the neighborhood and had come back to teach at her alma mater. Nothing had changed for me.

As a student in the hell that was this school, I had been chosen to work for the principal each morning so that I didn't have to be in the schoolyard. Being an SP student in the high-achieving class brought more terror and disdain than I could have expected. Being smart was not cool, and the students who were in SP were bullied mercilessly.

Returning to the school brought reminders of the jealousy, dislike, and mistreatment I had experienced as a student. This time, my fellow teachers made fun of my homemade clothing and my shy and quiet demeanor.

Every day during my work, the memories erupted. I would go home every day to the attic where I lived on the third floor of my parent's home and hate that my world was so small, limited, and depressing. Only a warm and friendly greeting from my grandmother each day and a hot dinner ready to eat with her helped me to stay in a healthy frame of mind.

The assistant principal, Ms. Miller, had taught both the new male teacher with the legal briefcase and me in middle school as our typing teacher. Yes, typewriting. Ms. Miller became a bigger part of both our lives on a day when we two new hires were passing her office simultaneously.

"Mr. Williams," she called out. "Do you have a minute?" "Yes," he replied.

I heard my name called before I went into the door for the stairwell upstairs. "Miss Taylor, do you have a class this period?"

I answered, "No, I have a prep period."

Right outside the main office, in the center hall, Ms. Miller took my hand in one of hers and Eric Williams' hand in her other hand. "I want to introduce you to each other," she said in the deep, commanding voice that rang of her refined, white-glove, Black-upper-class upbringing. "I think you two would make great friends, having both been students who have now come back here to teach."

I smiled. Eric Williams extended his hand, and we shook hands. I thanked Ms. Miller and left.

Later, Eric told me that he thought at first I was stuck up. I shared that I had thought he was, too.

Throughout our years working at the school together, we both rose to positions of authority as part of Ms. Miller's cabinet when she became principal. I worked as an administrator and teacher, and Eric became a dean of students. We did become friends. We would have lunch together, and I would share my stories of bad dates gone horrible. Eventually, he did attempt to have a date with me, but it fizzled.

As colleagues improving the quality of education and working in after-school initiatives, we both shared a fierce dedication to our students. A community initiative was brought to the school, and Ms. Miller chose Eric as the director of the program in the building. His most treasured project as part of this initiative was starting a basketball team. In a school with a high percentage of behavior problems and the typical challenges of working with students who are coming from challenging home environments, this team was a wonderful opportunity for these young men. I also worked in the after-school program. One day, Eric came to me and asked if I would start a cheerleader team.

"What?" I asked. "Cheerleaders? You are asking me to take girls who tear each other apart on the pre-scheduled Friday afternoon gang fights and make them cheerleaders?"

My reaction gave him a big laugh for a few minutes. When he stopped laughing and saw that I was not, he said seriously, "Yes."

I agreed because I saw how much this effort meant to him. *Here we go,* I thought nervously. I gathered the all-star girls I had in my classes. And together, Eric and I pulled off a winning basketball team and ass-kicking cheerleaders. Eric paid for the team's uniforms out of his salary, and I broke out my sewing machine and bought the material to make twenty cheerleader tops and skirts in one night. The other teachers might have jeered at my homemade clothes, but my sewing skills came in handy.

Eric pulled together some of the most difficult boys in the school and made them a team. He had rules, though. On game day, players had to wear a shirt, tie, and sport jacket. This custom went back to his days of attending a private school on a scholarship, where that attire was required every day. He felt that dressing formally created a sense of confidence and communicated to the less-than-supportive teachers in the school that these players could be better students with a little TLC.

The girls traveled together with the boy's team. Sometimes, while we were visiting schools kicking the crap out of their teams, their students would be in the locker room taking our belongings. Sometimes, we even had to run after the games, chased by the observers who didn't like watching our cheerleaders or getting beat in the game. But through all of the craziness, this good girl remained steady. Even though we were risking physical harm, the team spirit and camaraderie among our students was overwhelming.

What also started to become overwhelming was the tall, fair-skinned, curly haired, intelligent, and kind man who looked really good in his salmon suit and white buck shoes one day at a game. Somehow I watched my coworker more than the team playing. I let the impulse pass.

Building on this after-school experience, Eric approached me with an idea to start our own program as partners. We both desired to offer quality remedial services to children and adults on afternoons and weekends. So we began to talk for hours on the phone outlining our plan, which came into existence as The American Learning Institute. Purely as friends, we started ALI, Inc.

On the campus of my Lutheran church down the block was a tiny schoolhouse with six classrooms on the first floor and six in the basement. It looked like the schoolhouse from *Little House on the Prairie.* We negotiated an arrangement with the church to rent the building on Saturdays and summers. Eric was the president of the corporation, while I was the vice president, and it was a successful entity for many years.

My role was to create educational planning for remediation and to interface with instructors and parents as an educational director. We created flyers, and after-school each day, we walked the streets of our neighborhoods touting this innovative after school program. We hired teachers we knew, my brother and sister, and ALI, Inc. was born. We were a success. It was the second time we came together as a team.

This new initiative was exciting and adventurous. I marveled in following the lead of this kind, industrious, ambitious guy. ALI, Inc. brought us closer together and eventually down the aisle.

As I said, I eventually married the teacher with the big briefcase. My husband and I had a special bond of many shared experiences, both together and separately. We were both educators from Hollis, Queens. Separately, although we were years apart, we went to the same middle school, grew up in adjoining neighborhoods, and knew many of the same teachers. We even had the same middle school principal. Our paths were destined to cross. And my attraction to him and his work ethic reflected my upbringing.

We shared a love of teaching and working with young people. We both loved to impart knowledge so that a new generation could excel and find a path to a better way of life like we all hope to accomplish. I had always heard from my elders that I could go further in life because I had a college degree. And being the first person on both sides of my family to graduate from college, I was an example for my siblings and cousins. Eric had been told that education was freedom. It was the key to success, and it armed you with something that, no matter your circumstance, no one could take away from you.

Working close together brought us closer together. And at some point, being best friends turned into romance.

6

The Good Girl Serves Her Sunday Best

My observations of the relationships between the elder women in my household and their spouses contributed to my actions in numerous ways as a married woman. I learned that sometimes it was okay not to carry all of the worry, not to have to make every decision, and not to feel like I was alone in this world. What I observed in my house as a little girl and young woman was love, partnership, and friendship. As I look back now, I know that I also saw evidence of trust.

My role models were women who lived to be wives. They appeared to be happy in their lives. I wanted this "happy." And when I grew up, I had this happy. It was not a delirious, unrealistic happy. My happy came from finding a partner for life, which was a man with a vision and ambition, a man who was brilliant and who, with every conversation, taught me something interesting. It was not so long after we met that a whirlwind courtship of two years came, followed by marriage.

When I think about what I was looking for in a spouse, it all came down to a combination of the men I grew up around. I wanted someone who was hardworking. Also, I was in need of someone to help me see my beauty. I eventually found him. It took me until my twenties when I met my husband to realize I had freckles.

"Hey," I said one day, "I need to get something for these acne spots I have had forever, even as a little girl."

He replied, "Wow, you have freckles!"

"No, I don't," I said adamantly.

"Yes, you do!"

"No, I don't," I said again. How could I have freckles?

"Yes, you really do."

"Really?" I finally considered that he was telling me the truth. "Really?"

"Yes. And they are beautiful."

At that light-bulb moment, I finally shared with him the hurtful label the kids had placed on me for over a decade because of my freckles. That insult lost its sting for me when I realized how my husband saw me.

I recall one New Year's Eve I spent with my grandmother. We had a ritual: LAYS® potato chips and sparkling cider served in long-stemmed wine glasses was our menu of choice. The ball dropped, and my grandmother looked at me and said, "Tees, I know you are tired of sitting here with me on New Year's Eve."

I responded, "I love it!"

"This is going to be your year." She said that every year.

But my grandmother was more adamant about her prediction this time. Personally, I wasn't so confident. I was in my early twenties, working as a teacher and living in my family's attic.

Well, it turned out that my grandmother was right. That new year did bring the man who was to be my husband. Our courtship was full of experiences that reminded me of the times when my aunt exposed me to culture, music, theater, and the arts.

Eric and I went to Studio 54 and danced next to Frank Perdue, known as the "Chicken King" for his work with Purdue Farms. I saw Matthew Broderick in his first off-off-Broadway premiere. Eric and I spent Saturdays in Manhattan exploring SoHo and Greenwich Village. We ate at cafés and visited art shows. One Saturday, he took me to the most expensive store I had ever entered—Bergdorf Goodman.

Besides the excitement of these experiences, I felt nerves and anxiety when with him. He was tall and impressive, highly educated, ambitious, and strong. He walked into any venue like he belonged there. He would grab my hand and hold it tight to calm me down. I swallowed hard to look confident while my shyness was eating me up inside. Listening to his plans, goals, and ambitions filled me with something I never had. Hope and a future.

I was not making the assumption that I would be a part of his future, but it was the first time I heard anyone talking about it. I never doubted that he would achieve everything he was working towards. He spoke definitively and with conviction. Then, the time came when he became interested in my life and goals. Oh, the excitement!

Two things were major factors in our relationship: shopping and food. It didn't surprise me that we shared long talks about every subject over a good meal, and my husband loved a good meal. I learned that he was, like me, the one who didn't fit into the family unit. Like me, he was taller, smarter, and more creative than those around him. He was a misunderstood visionary.

My husband told me that the only person in his life who understood him and accepted him completely was his grandmother. The same was true for me growing up. My grandmother was my friend, my savior, and my champion. My husband and I bonded on this similarity among many others. Our grandmothers had so many similarities that the coincidence was almost eerie.

Eric always spoke of his grandmother, Margaret, with love, satisfaction, and pure joy.

"My grandmother protected me and made sure I was treated fairly," he said. "Her nickname for me was 'Precious.' Even when I was obstinate. When I wouldn't take my hat off in church, she shielded me from strangers who tried to make me take it off. She was the one person in the world who got me."

I felt the same about my grandmother whom I called "Katin."

I remember the first time I invited Eric over to my childhood home for our traditional Sunday dinner when Katin made lemon meringue pie. The menu for the day was Southern cuisine: fried chicken, mac and cheese, greens, cornbread muffins, and candy sweets. Eric arrived at my house shortly after I returned from church, where I had been the church usher for that service. Church had run late, so I didn't have time to take off my usher attire of uninterrupted white stockings, shoes, dress, gloves, and a doily on my head.

Up to that point, Eric had never seen me outside of work at the middle school. My appearance was a surprise.

"You remind me of my grandmother who was a Pentecostal minister." His grandmother had taken him to church when he was a boy, so thankfully, he was very familiar with my role as an usher.

"Katin" I called out to my grandmother. "We're coming up." Eric followed me up the long flight of stairs and into the kitchen to be formally introduced to my favorite person in the world. Katin was finishing up the chicken and told Eric that he was free to have a seat.

"Mrs. Craft, I'm Eric," he said as he extended his hand to shake hers.

"Welcome, Eric," she replied.

"Something smells good. Teresa has told me what a great cook you are. Thank you for having me," he added.

"We welcome everyone for a meal," she said with a cautious smile.

Katin was friendly. She was also highly protective of me, which explained her cautious behavior.

"I'm going to change my clothes," I said, and I told Eric to wait in the living room. Before I finished changing, I heard the door downstairs open, and my mother, father, sister, and brother stomped up the stairs. Sunday dinner meant that we all ate together in the kitchen.

I heard voices and introductions happening through the thin walls. A lot of talking was going on, and my brother had turned on sports, which would provide a common theme for discussion amongst them, alleviating any silent moments.

When I came out of the bedroom, having changed into a dress, my mother and grandmother were setting the table. I also heard talking, laughing, and the football game on the television. Eric, my father, and my brother were talking sports and being very loud and animated about it. Eric was a former athlete. Having played almost every sport, he lived and breathed televised games.

"Hey, what's going on in here?" I asked as I entered the living room.

"Your dad and brother are rooting for the wrong team!" Eric said jokingly. They shared his humor.

"It's going to be too crowded in here today," I said, already seeing not enough room in the tiny second-floor kitchen. I suggested that Eric and I eat upstairs in the attic apartment. "Is that okay?" I asked my mother and grandmother. They both said yes. With that, I led him up to my attic apartment. He commented on how bright it was and that he, too, was living in the attic at his home.

He took a seat in one of my two wicker chairs, and I slid over a small wooden table. This and my sofa were remnants of my great-grandmother's furniture that I had painted and recovered after her death. Louver doors separated the front of the attic, which had one small window and my dresser and bed. I didn't want Eric to see my bed because I was embarrassed for him to see that I slept on a box spring. I was saving for a mattress that I would buy with my first credit card.

I went down the stairs to the kitchen, and I grabbed two plates. As I had been trained, I filled the first plate for him.

"Did you ask him what part of the chicken he likes?' my grandmother asked. "No."

"Ask him."

I went halfway up the stairs and called, "White or dark meat?"

"I eat anything," he replied. Later, I found that to be true.

I returned with a plate of food and went back downstairs to fill mine. I turned the station to CD 101.9, an all-cool-jazz station. We ate, talked, and laughed.

"This is the best meal I have ever had," he exclaimed. "Did you cook this?"

"I helped, but I know how to make the whole meal myself."

Then came the Sunday best. This week, it was sky-high lemon meringue pie. I cut a huge slice of pie and placed it on the end table. He controlled himself long enough to wait until I came back up with mine.

As our friendship progressed, Eric told me that being at my house on that day sharing our Sunday best reminded him of his days living with his grandmother, whose tenant cooked Sunday dinners for all the other tenants in the house. When he was a little boy at his grandmother's house, Eric would sit for hours talking with his disabled aunt, who couldn't get up and down the stairs, just like Katin.

Eric's grandmother had been a highly respected evangelist in the Pentecostal faith. After services on Sundays, dinner was served around a huge table to clergy, including his grandmother. Because he never separated from her, Eric was allowed to sit and eat with them.

"My grandmother treated me well and made sure I got the piece of fried chicken I liked the most!" he recalled.

Our mutual love and respect for our grandmothers formed the beginning of the many personal links that he and I uncovered. It was so easy to have him in my home and around my family. He understood the importance of my grandmother in my life and considered the time I spent with her a blessing. He came to love her, too. He brought her gifts, made her laugh, and always praised her food. He called her "Mrs. Craft," which was her married name.

"Mrs. Craft," he would say, "I will eat anything you make for me!" Their relationship grew from his love of her food and her observation of his love for me.

The day came when my grandmother said to him, "Call me Katin." Her invitation was a mark of acceptance and understanding of what was growing between my future husband and me. Katin was inviting him into the family even before he asked to join it.

Eric seemed to feel and desire even at this early

stage the kind of love that filled my home, the kind of love that my mother and grandmother taught me to scrub into a floor or sew into a hemline or bake into a lemon meringue pie. He told me after our marriage that when I served him his slice of pie that first Sunday dinner, right at that moment he knew he had to marry me.

So when Katin invited him to call her by name like one of the family, Eric looked at me with a grateful smile that said, I've found a home. He had. And he knew that wherever I went with him, I could make the same kind of home for him, filled with the same kind of love and care, right down to the Sunday best.

7

Making of the Good Boy

I wonder if everyone has a soul mate. Has the universe or a greater being deemed that one person, in particular, will be your perfect partner in life? Does one special person have such similarities in experiences that you feel a sensory connection with your first touch, kiss, or conversation?

Perhaps there is no rule of how and where you meet the person who shares your life or how that moment unfolds. My first meeting at school with my husband was not exactly a meeting of the minds. I was cautious about meeting new people. He appeared to be friendly and engaging, but nothing

73

about him said to me, *This is your soulmate.*

At first, Eric and I didn't know the extent of the experiences that we shared. I never guessed that I would marry this tall man with his athlete's physique and his confident, strong, intimidating demeanor. I assumed that men didn't cry. Tough men especially never cried. I didn't know that this man who was impressive, brilliant, tough, and at times even a little scary, could share stories with me about his life that would bring us both to tears.

Once, he told me, "T, there were times in my life when I felt I was alone in this world. Every day was a battle to survive, and I had to be an animal."

Looking into the eyes of the man who I had come to know as a gentle giant, the life he described to me just didn't match the person I knew. I couldn't picture him behaving differently than the way I had seen him behave near me at school and with his team. But he had reason to learn to fend for himself. He had known pain in his childhood.

"Think of being three years old and playing with your toy trucks happily on the living room floor," he remembered. "Imagine seeing your mom walk past you with a suitcase, heading for the door."

"What did you do?" I asked through tears. My tender heart easily felt his pain.

"I just remember getting up to hold onto her coat, thinking she was taking me with her to the park or the store, and then being swept up and held back by my dad," he said. "I think I reached out, crying like a little boy would for his mom to hold him. I never saw her again."

When his parents were together, he had lived in a nice, neat house and spent days at the park playing. He showed me photos of these happy times of him and his mother. How could he have known as he played with his toys on the floor that his home would fall apart?

Recalling this tragic moment caused tears to stream down his face. The explanation he heard to explain his mother's departure was that she left to pursue her career.

"My mom was from a wealthy Boston family. I guess she was a maverick for her time. She had a relationship with a Black man during the 1950s when interracial marriage was illegal," he explained.

His father was a tough Marine. From the stories Eric told me, his father was harsh and sometimes cruel. Being a single father in the 1950s, when single fathers were as rare as interracial marriages, was impossible if you were going to earn a living. So in the blink of an eye, his father packed Eric's belongings and took him to Philadelphia to live with his grandmother.

Eric had so many good qualities. He was brilliant and handsome and charming. But what actually drew me to him was that he loved and cared for his grandmother. His best quality grew from the deep pain of separation and loss.

"I would spend the weekdays living with my grandmother, and my dad would come and get me on the weekends or stay there and visit. I missed my dad. Over time, my missing him turned into anger at him and my mom both."

"Did anyone ever take the time to talk about your mom or mention seeing or speaking with her?" I asked.

"No. Never," he answered abruptly.

I didn't understand at the time that pain like his doesn't just disappear. I didn't know that mother-lessness chafes deep in the heart and looks always for another source of love. I thought that a faithful wife might heal the wound that an absent mother made.

Despite the pain of losing his mother, Eric found that life with his grandmother was happy in a different, new way. His grandmother owned a three-story house with roomers on the top two floors. Being the only child in the house, Eric got more than enough attention, and he ran up and down between the floors every day. I could imagine his boyhood there because it sounded like my own early childhood, running upstairs to visit my grandparents.

His grandmother warned Eric to stay within the gate of her small yard outside the house, just as I had been warned. One fateful day, he did what a typical little boy would do when his ball bounced into the street. He ran after it. A car struck him.

"I was lucky I wasn't hurt. I was also lucky that my grandmother was too happy I was all right to be mad that I broke her rule," he recalled. "My dad came down that weekend, and I was happy he was there."

I thought of young Eric, becoming accustomed to loss as a regular occurrence. After the permanent loss of his mother, he would have to say goodbye to his father over and over. I wondered what that did to his small heart. I wondered how he stood it when his father had to leave to take the bus back to New York.

Eric turned to the people around him for company and comfort.

"I had people to talk to all the time. One was my aunt, my grandmother's cousin. She was in a wheelchair, and she stayed on the second floor. The other was a man who cooked for my grandmother and most everyone in the house." This man, a cook, created the Sunday best dinners Eric remembered so fondly.

Eventually, Eric's father remarried and sent for Eric to move back from Philly to New York again. Though Eric missed his grandmother and took some time to adjust to his father's strictness again, the move led to a happy chance that made all the difference to his future.

One Sunday at Eric's church, a philanthropist came to the service to announce that he was giving two scholarships for private school to the most qual-ified students he found. Immediately, Eric's father went home to get the huge book he kept full of all the newspaper articles, accolades, and awards Eric had received for sports and academics. Eric received one of the two scholarships.

From then on, Eric always dressed in the preppy attire that he learned to accept during his private and Ivy League education. His clothing said that he had class, education, and a professional deportment. He was exceptionally well-spoken and well-versed in nearly any topic. He was brilliant, forward-thinking, and always setting higher goals to achieve. Private school molded him into a man who could succeed and did.

However, the softness and ease of private school life after the hardship of our middle school didn't transform Eric into a wimp. He still looked at the world as a battleground. He told me of fights at sum-mer camp. "I had at least thirty-five fights," he boast-ed, laughing.

"What? Why?" I asked. I couldn't imagine fighting so much. After all, I had spent most of my energy in middle school and high school, remaining invisible so that I wouldn't have to fight. I remembered the soda can top claws of the thugs at my school and shuddered.

"Didn't take anything from anyone," he explained. "I remembered what my dad told me one day when I was around ten or eleven years old, 'Other than me and your grandmother, you have no one else in this world. Life is war. Anytime you leave your house, you must be ready for battle.' He was serious when he told me that. I took it seriously."

These statements were huge windows into a man who took pride in being a pillar of strength. Eric did everything he could to avoid showing weakness. But obviously, he did have weaknesses. I was one of them. If I hurt, he hurt. If I cried, a look came into his eyes that said, I can't take this pain, and I have to do anything I can to fix it.

He took pride in protecting me, in rescuing his damsel in distress. He saw me, living in my third-floor attic, as his Rapunzel, the long-tressed princess he would steal away from her tower. I believed in that vision of us.

I felt comfort and bliss in knowing that I had such a strong and caring partner in life. While I was with him, I never felt afraid. I worried very little because I believed that my very own prince could take care of anything. I was sure that I had found the "good boy" to match my "good girl."

Part II
The Perfect Wife

Interlude with a Ho

You're a ho. The lying, scheming, murdering-kind-of ho. The calculating, cold-hearted, manipulating-type-of ho. The big-breasted, skanky, stealing-a-man-and-more-type-of ho. The kind of ho who takes lives, kills marriages, wrecks homes, and makes children fatherless. You are the ho who has no conscience who plays on the weak, the wandering, the lost, the balding, the aging, the horny.

You live to fuck and you do it well. Your lips perform CPR on organs gone limp. You might think I would wish you dead—no, I wish you life, a very, very long life with all the pain, suffering, hurt, loss, disappointment, and treachery you introduced into mine.

I know your birthday, so I might just send you a card. I know the lingerie you wear, so I'll keep the brand in mind. I know your favorite shoe store, the trampy clothes you wear, where you eat, what you drive, what you drink. I know the words you whispered in my husband's ear. I've read your ignorant dialect.

I know how you love to spend lavishly—on Fendi, Gucci, Louis Vuitton, Prada, and BeBe. You drink cheap wine to match your cheap weave, and you were well trained in your craft on how to sit next to a wife and lie, and lie, and lie with no thought of her revenge. So, I know you'll hump anything with a dollar in hand. So, I know now what you saw in my man. We even met—before I knew who you really were. My lying, cheating, pathetic, broken, scheming husband actually brought us together. I didn't know you were the ho, and I didn't know he had lost his mind. I never thought he'd sink so low. So, you sat next to me and talked to me and told me how you knew so much about me—you loved my hair, I was so pretty, I had a wonderful husband—how he was such a great business partner for you. You even asked me, "What can you tell me to help me understand him more?" You pushed to meet my children, and you chose to sit your ho ass down with them.

And therein lies the reason for why I wrote this book.

This book is for wives who have met the ho and lost the battle. This book is for the wives who have not met the ho but feel she might be lurking close. This book is for the wives who battled the ho, won, and have watched the skank slither away. This book is for the daughters who one day will love, trust, and marry but won't lose to the ho because they will know the signs, smell the stank they exude, hear the words that mean they're near, and stop the reign of the ho over their men.

8

Mr. Magic

During our courtship, I heard an R&B song called "Magic Man." One of the lines of the song said, "I'm your magic man...just take my hand... I'll make all your dreams come true." Every card my husband would send me, he signed "Mr. Magic." And rightfully so. He climbed the flights of stairs in a two-family, three-generation house all the way to the attic, and he said he found an empress waiting there to be rescued. He called me "Empress" until he died. After my grandmother passed, he truly became my knight in shining armor.

He was my Mr. Magic.

So many times during the time we dated, Eric and I drove into the city and spent the day walking, talking, and dreaming. We browsed in Bergdorf Goodman, Bonwit Teller, and Barney's, stores I hadn't known existed before these wonderful Saturdays. Many times, we found our way to 43rd Street and entered a building that looked as if it said, *Here is where geniuses gather.* This was the Princeton Club of New York. Because Eric had attended Princeton University, he was a member.

One afternoon found me in Manhattan having brunch there. As I walked towards the P-Club, I admired the stately building on its secluded New York City street that sunshine never quite fully lit. The darkness of the street made it feel eerie, just as I imagined that quaint streets in London must have felt. I heard whipping sounds on windy days from the waving of the American flag and the black and orange Princeton University flag. Entering this building as if I belonged was exhilarating.

Just past the revolving door, a stately-looking gentleman said, "Good day," and pointed us towards the coat check. Coats were not allowed in the dining area. Neither was money. After our first lunch together there, the waiter had taken a small white card with a photo of the club on it to pay the check. Apparently, this was a place where the exchange of cash would have cheapened the dining experience. Many years later, having married a Princeton man, I had my own card with my name on it.

But this Saturday, Eric and I didn't eat in the downstairs dining room. We took the elevator straight up to the second floor, where the waiters wore white gloves and the chairs were draped in silk.

"Why are we up here? Isn't this really expensive?" Without answering, he smiled and grabbed my hand as we walked to a reserved seat by the window.

Whatever my meal was for the day, I can't remember. I was so enamored of the beauty around me that Saturday in September, from the wind in the flags outside to the formal splendor of the room where I sat on silk. Surrounded by intelligence and style, I felt that I was experiencing a day I would always remember. And I was right.

When we finished eating and talking, in one swift move Eric knelt on the floor. I thought something had dropped, and I started looking under the table. But just as if I were watching a movie in slow motion, I saw what was happening. We were at eye level, me leaning down from my seat and my future husband on his knee.

"What? Why are you on the floor? Are you sick?" I asked in frantic disbelief. He said nothing, just stared at me and took my hand.

If I told you that I heard him say, "Will you marry me?" I would be lying. I heard nothing around me. I felt disconnected from my body as surely as if my soul had flown out the window.

When my ears finally popped, Eric was laughing,

and this time amongst a room of laughter, I heard him say, "Marry me!"

There was no ring in his hand. I didn't need one to accept him. Three decades ago, we were on a teacher's salary. The ring would follow in time from a Sunday excursion I took one day to TSS, which was the Costco of the eighties. Tucked away in a jewelry case full of shiny, cheap-looking chains and earrings was a small section marked ESTATE SALE. And there it was—a solitaire diamond ring for $900. For our pockets, that price seemed like $9,000.

I called and told Eric, "I found it!" There was only one "it" I could mean with that level of excitement in my voice.

"At TSS?" he asked.

"Yep," I replied.

"No. Not doing this. We will go to Tiffany's after payday."

"Too late. I put a $20 deposit on the ring to hold it. I love it, and it's mine. One day," I added, "You can buy me what you want." Thank God for layaway.

So now I was engaged. I was happy and sad at the same time. I held the news inside for a while until I could decide what to do about my beloved grandmother. I had lived with her from age fourteen, beginning the night my grandfather died, and now things would change. Katin and I were glued at the hip.

I loved and adored her, and out of all the others in my home, Katin got me. She understood the strange little girl who was afraid of the world and so different from her parents and siblings. She always told me that I was special and that one day all that I did for her would come back to me in tons of blessings. I never thought that way. There was nothing I wouldn't do for her.

Katin was the lead manager of teaching me how to take care of a home and a husband, how to cook, clean, and shop. She was the greatest contributor to fostering a sense of advocacy, patience, and kindness towards others. The night I moved upstairs to stay with her, I slept on my grandfather's side. I felt more secure and comforted than ever. Not until my great-grandmother, Sophie, passed away when I was seventeen had I moved upstairs to the third-floor attic on my own.

I had decorated my two-room apartment on the third floor in lime green, white, and orange. I painted my great-grandmother's old tables orange, covered her old sofa with an orange tablecloth, and bought a lime green shag rug for the bedroom floor. Then I threw a wallpapering party one Saturday. My girlfriends from high school and middle school and I papered the attic in glossy white paper adorned with giant green leaves. The pay? My grandmother's delicious spaghetti with homemade Italian sauce.

Even living on different floors, Katin and I were still inseparable. I preferred to have dinner and cook with her and watch our favorite shows to being downstairs with my family. My grandmother suffered from severe arthritis and a thyroid problem which kept an unhealthy amount of weight on her 5'5" frame. Because her arthritis restricted her from ever venturing downstairs, we made her life on the second floor as happy as we could.

So, the thought of moving away from her left me torn. I wanted to embark on my new life as wife to a wonderful man. I couldn't wait to step into a role I had been groomed to fulfill for most of my life, the role of the good wife. But at the same time, I wanted to stay with my precious grandmother.

So, I waited as long as I could to break the news that one day soon I would have to leave her. I walked into the kitchen, where she sat each morning and had her coffee. I sat across from her in a chair, not at the table, which was our daily ritual.

"Katin, I have something to tell you," I said.

"Are you pregnant?" she asked. Unwed pregnancy, as you can guess, was the greatest fear she must have had. I heard my relatives speak of it with disdain in my house growing up. Getting pregnant before marriage was not what "good girls" did.

"No!" I said with an anger that I had never shown towards my grandmother.

"Then what's wrong?" she replied.

With tears pouring down my face, I half cried and half shouted, "I'm engaged!"

With a combination of relief, joy, and no signs

of sadness, she looked up towards the sky and said, "Praise God! Thank you Jesus!" and held out her arms to hug me.

From that point on, we were off to the races. The target date for the wedding was April 10, 1982. The year of planning passed quickly.

My wedding day was going to be a dream come true with formal attire, bridesmaid dresses from a notable, bridal boutique, men in black ties and tails, long black stretch limos, and the best catering hall in the neighborhood. The search for my dress took me to one of the stores my mother and I had frequently passed on our Saturday Manhattan excursions, a store where my aunt had once worked and from which she had brought clothes home for me regularly as a little girl—Arnold Constable. It was the equivalent of Bergdorf Goodman but more understated. With my mother and aunt in tow, I went to the bridal boutique there. It looked like a dream with all of the white and diamonds. Everything sparkled, and gowns flowed off every hook onto the white carpeted floors.

To my surprise, a tall, beautiful, brown-skinned woman came from the back and welcomed us to have a seat on the plushest sofas I had ever seen. She sat across from us and asked what I wanted to look like on my wedding day. That thought had never crossed my mind. I only had one reference image, and it was the photo of my mother and father at their wedding party on their wedding day.

My mother's veil had been long and lacy. It flowed well beyond her dress. She had a high-laced collar and lace sleeves. She was a vision standing next to my father who wore a fitted tuxedo just like the eight groomsmen standing next to him. My mother's bridesmaids wore floral crowns and short veils that touched the tops of their chins.

I wanted so badly to look like her. Within minutes of describing this picture to the saleswoman, she emerged from the back with a lace and off-white, satin gown. It was covered in lace to the neck with lace sleeves and touches of lace on the satin skirt.

"Come try this one on," she said.

Stepping into the layers of fabric and French lace felt magical. It was like nothing I had ever worn, notwithstanding the fact that I had sewn most of my clothes from my teen years on because I couldn't afford to buy them. Wearing that dress for the first time truly was a Cinderella moment. Just as Cinderella had done, I had scrubbed the floors on my hands and knees in my house, and now here I was, fit for a ball. I walked out to show my mother and aunt.

They both stood up with tears in their eyes.

"Teresa!" my aunt screamed. "This is it! This is the one! Isn't it Sophie?" she asked my mother.

My mother was not an emotional person. She wasn't a hugger. She simply asked me, "Do you like it?"

"Yes, Ma."

"Then get it," she said.

In all of this fantasy, we hadn't asked the most important question.

"How much does this cost?" I anxiously asked.

The saleswoman studied me shrewdly, "Well, your sleeves are a bit too short, so we'll have to order the gown with extra-long sleeves. There will be additional shipping charges from Paris, but we will absorb those."

What—wait—where? Stop! Paris? Paris, France? I was so taken aback that I didn't hear anything for a long pause. I had a dress on that was made in Paris?

"How much? How much?" I timidly asked again, almost in a whisper.

"$1,200.00 before tax."

In that silence and frozen-faced moment, a voice responded without hesitation.

"She will take it," my mother said without a blink of an eye. And that was that.

To put things into perspective, my formal, black-tie wedding in a beautiful and catered facility for one hundred twenty guests, limos, and church fees cost $3,400. For my parents, a city-employed administrator and a medallion taxicab owner, this amount was a mint.

I remember how impressive it felt to walk out of the store with a huge Arnold Constable box in hand. Everyone who saw me knew what was inside and smiled at me.

After listening that evening to the price of my gown and wedding costs, Eric said, "T, if that's the dress of your dreams, then we will pay for it. Not your parents. And the flowers, too."

Little did I know that this promise introduced a pattern of how we would deal with challenges as a team. Together.

9

Two Rolls Royces

My wedding day was surreal. I felt over-whelmed and confused about what I was about to do. I knew I wanted to marry my husband, but I was torn because I didn't want to leave my grandmother. This thought had run constantly through my mind for a year from the day I had sat in the kitchen and told her that I was engaged. Of course, she was so happy for me. She called it an answered prayer because of how much I deserved to be happy. I had been such a good girl all of my life.

Saturday, the day of the wedding day, came, and I woke up to lots of talk and panic. The night before, the limo company had called and said they would give us a deal on a Rolls Royce to replace my limo. My mother and I screamed in sync, "No!" We were at our limit because of stress, and we didn't want to make any changes to the plans.

Running downstairs from the attic, I saw my grandmother all dressed in white gloves and a beautiful dress with her hair pressed and curled and makeup applied, sitting by the kitchen window. She was ready. Because of her arthritis, however, she couldn't come to the ceremony.

Our neighbor from across the street was going to keep her company during the ceremony. After church, the two Rolls Royce cars would take Eric and me back to the house so that we could go upstairs to hug, kiss, and cry with her before the reception. It was clear, even though I was now married, that my heart and commitment to Katin would stay the same.

Finally, my mother assisted me with my gown, and the flowers arrived. I took a huge white orchid and pinned it on my grandmother's dress. That was the first photo in my wedding album. Everything proceeded to go well. Before I kissed my grandmother goodbye, she called my mother and me to the window. She said that two huge cars pulled up, but they weren't black stretch limos.

My wedding day was April 10, 1982. Minimal signs remained of the record blizzard that had hit on Tuesday, April 6, 1982, which is famously known as the "Blizzard of '82." On that beautiful April morning, my brother and father were chopping up ice along the curve. Other than the ice, blue skies and sunshine prevailed. Drowning out the sounds of ice being chopped against concrete were the screams of crazed women yelling out of the second-floor windows.

"Ma! Ma!" I screamed. "The company didn't listen to you! Ma! Ma!" I yelled, running through the house like a wild woman.

"What? What's wrong? Oh, no..." my grandmother started to cry. "I knew it was too good to be true! He's not showing up, is he? That %$^&&! I'm going to kill him! He's standing my Tis' up on her wedding day? Soph!" (short for my mother who was Sophie), "Get him on the phone. Now!"

"No, Ma," my mother replied. "It's not about him. The company didn't listen."

All of this dialogue took place in high-pitched, angry speech that vibrated throughout our three-tiered, family home. it could be heard from the attic where I lived down to the second floor where Katin lived and ending up on the first floor where my mother, father, sister, and brother lived.

Excited screaming began again as I kissed my grandmother goodbye, lifted my gown, ran down the long set of stairs, out the side door, and followed my mother to the first floor.

Stomping down the two flights of stairs, my mother was racing me to get in my father's face about the two Rolls Royces pulling up to the front of our freshly watered sidewalk and curb.

She must have dialed the limo company by osmosis. Before I could lift my veil and gown through the door, fire was going into that phone.

"Robert," she called my father. "Robert… Robert…" My father came inside from policing the yard and curb outside. Cool, calm, and smiling, he said,

"What, Sophie? I did what a father has the right to do for his oldest daughter, who has always been a good girl!" My father had secretly called the limo company, requesting that they replace the two limos with two Rolls Royce cars. Mine was cream. Eric's was a beautiful blue.

I fell into my father's arms. Excitedly, we all ran inside to get ready for the wedding.

Within the hour, the photographer had arrived and photographed my wedding gown which was laid out on my grandmother's bed. Next to it rested my grandmother's pearls which were the "something old" I was given on that day. A garter took the place of something blue, and my Stuart Weitzman lace pumps were definitely something new.

After the photos, my family all bolted out the door to get into the waiting Rolls. My sister flowed in yellow silk and matching elbow-length gloves and yellow veil. My mother, in violet satin brocade with a chin-length veil, entered the blue Rolls. My brother drove the family car the three blocks away down to the church where I had been a Girl Scout, Sunday school member, and later a business tenant. My father helped me down the steps and into the waiting cream-colored Rolls. All of the neighbors out on the block applauded as we all pulled off to head for the ceremony.

When we pulled up in front of the church, crowds of people were standing outside in amazement to see not one but two Rolls Royce cars. I recall stepping out of the car to a throng of neighbors and relatives who lined the walk to the steps of the chapel. I felt like a star. Cameras were flashing like I was a celebrity. And on that day, the Taylor family of 200th Street, who stood out because of the strict rules, tight reigns, and private lives they led. The Taylor family, who raised their children among a crumbling neighborhood quickly succumbing to the crack epidemic, stood out brilliantly. Some of the onlookers came up to look inside, wish me well, and get a peek inside a car they had never seen—two people I didn't know.

I stepped out to greet my wedding party lined up the stairs, my sister and mistress of honor, and my bridesmaids in spring green dresses slightly blowing in the wind. Green veils to the chin. The wedding party proceeded down the aisle. Doors closed. The minute my father and I got to the top of the stairs, I looked at him, and he was crying hysterically, like huge tears with uncontrollable shaking and crying. He was crying so much that someone had to hold him up until the doors opened. By the time they opened, there stood two people: a bride in a beautiful antique white Arnold Constable gown from France and a man in a perfectly fitted black tuxedo crying like someone had died.

My father and I stepped forward. Doors opened. Guests stood at their feet. My father extended his arm. I held on tight. We turned to look at each other before the first step, and, together, we walked arm in arm with tears flowing all the way down the aisle. In fact, he never stopped crying through the ceremony.

We cried down the aisle. We cried during the ceremony. The guests cried. We cried down the aisle, and at the reception, we were still crying. It was one big cry fest!

"Who gives this woman to this man?" asked the minister.

In an almost inaudible voice, shaking and quiet, father said, "I do." My mother had to step up to help him to the pew.

The ceremony was traditional, with little deviation from what would be expected. Eric and I had a Christian ceremony with all the usual vows except for one phrase that I specifically objected to saying, which was an issue with the minister. I wouldn't say "obey."

It was important for me not to say "obey" in the ceremony because it made me feel unequal in the relationship. Oddly, that choice probably went against some of what defined me as the good girl. I also think it was an indication of the part of me that was defiant and felt that I wanted equal rights and status in our marriage.

The extremely emotional ceremony ended with the trip back down the aisle, this time on the arm of my new husband but with the tears flowing just as hard as on the trip up.

The wedding party piled into the two Rolls Royce cars. How different the world looked through the windows of a Rolls! Decaying Linden Boulevard, the main street through my neighborhood, looked less tattered and more pristine.

It was a magical day that mirrored that fairy tale night when a prince found the golden slipper and rescued Cinderella. I was Cinderella, and my Prince rescued me.

So, having come out of an environment that was conducive to nothing but trouble, being the good girl paid off.

10

After the "I Do's"

Life runs in strange circles. As Papa's first grand-child, whom he called "Tierce" (pronounced like 'lease'), I married a man who was a lot like him. That likeness was another reason that I felt the universe had brought him into my life. Eric's story was my grandpa's story.

My grandpa had been the product of an inter-racial relationship. His mother, my great-grand-mother, was German, and I was named after her. My grandpa's father was a Bermudian seaman who had been lost at sea. The similarities were astounding. Eric, too, had a White mother and Black father who had been at sea and who was also a Marine.

My family is a hodgepodge of ethnicities. So the day my future husband, this half-Black, half-White man with his fair, almost-white skin and his straight hair slicked back, came to have Sunday dinner, no one batted an eye. He referred occasionally to this non-reaction during our marriage because he immediately felt comfortable around my family after they just took him in.

My husband always reminded me of my Papa. He was kind. He was my protector. He looked out for me. He thought that I could do anything and told me so, and he did everything he could to make all of my dreams come true. He was the reason I had dreams. I didn't dare to dream about the future before I met my husband. I couldn't see life beyond the day or the week in front of me.

I didn't know that I was really smart and that I should not be ashamed of being smart. I didn't know that being tall was a good thing. Eric didn't allow me to bend over to hide my height. I didn't know that having many ethnicities in my DNA made me beautiful and special. Eric helped me understand and accept that the freckles in my skin were what he called beauty marks and that they were nothing to hide.

I had finally found someone who saw the world as I saw it. My husband and I came from adjoining neighborhoods and held similar positions in our families, being smart and tall and looking different from the rest. We shared similar values and had respect for advanced education and giving back to our communities. Most of all, we loved working with young people and helping them to see their potential.

In him, I found a friend who laughed out loud at my stories and hung onto my every word. The term sounds like such a cliché, but we were *soulmates*. I found comfort in him, and I saw that he really cared about knowing who I was and understanding my background. We felt like strangers where we were. We had both grown up in the same neighborhood but really didn't belong there.

In my lifetime, I have had many supporters: my mother, my father, my sister, my brother, my grandparents, and today, even my children. But despite the turns of life and the hurt and pain that have come to me in recent years, during the years of our marriage, my husband was unequivocally the most instrumental booster and the biggest cheerleader I had. He told me that I was not strange or weird but exceptional. He did everything in his power to be my Mr. Magic and make my dreams come true.

Our marriage was successful not only because we loved each other but also because we respected each other. My husband encouraged my personal growth, my pursuit of advanced degrees, and my business ventures, and he was ready to back his supportive words with financing. In this tough, harsh, cruel, sexist, dangerous world, just knowing that I had a real-life warrior standing at the foot of my bed reassured me. What my husband and I had was comforting, exciting, educational, loving, and special. He was my best friend and my dedicated mentor. Most of all, he helped me to realize that I was perfection, just the way I was.

For many years we ran our educational business, ALI, Inc., together. When Eric went to Wall Street, I ran it alone until we sold it. It still holds a place in my heart for how close my husband and I were in our drive, determination, and teamwork at its founding. He taught me how to turn a thought into a conglomerate.

My husband was a big man, both in stature and in personality. He was worldly and educated, an Ivy Leaguer, a Wall Street maverick, a law school student, and a collector of fine books, art, artifacts, and paintings. His interests were as diverse as his ethnicity. The last reading material he started included *War and Peace, The Financial Times,* and *How to Read Egyptian.*

Before children came, we both looked forward to the weekends, when we would go on adventures like a long drive upstate, a trip to Barnes & Noble bookstore to browse for hours, or a walk through the city's SoHo galleries with dinner to follow. Sundays, we spent in church or looking at homes, planning our next moves. Sunday evenings, Eric read *Barron's* to prepare for the opening bell on Wall Street while I read on the other couch.

My husband loved the movies, and we went to several every month. We both loved clothes and bargain shopping. He valued family highly, even creating unique traditions to strengthen it. One beautiful tradition he created for our family was going to DC every year to see the cherry blossoms together. He was not the type of man who spent every spare moment on the golf course making deals. When his firm had Christmas parties and other events, he couldn't wait to come home and be with his family. He truly strove for a work/life balance and put family first.

The early years of our marriage were like a splendid journey to the unknown, filled with anticipation and hope. Our nickname became "The Jeffersons" after the TV show, a nickname coined by my father because Eric and I made good investment decisions in property, moved up to a high rise, and experienced career success professionally. Our success appeared in the cars we drove, the clothes we wore, and the companies that my husband joined. Life was happy and adventurous and rewarding as he and I saw our hard work and teamwork and education pay off in numerous ways. We stayed on the path to surpassing our parents' financial successes by far, and all along, we kept our own family running like a well-oiled machine.

One day, after I had been married for quite a while, I was sitting in a restaurant and chatting with several other women as we all waited for school dismissal to pick up our children. Valentine's Day was coming up, and two of the six of us were discussing rituals for this special day. These women talked about sexy lingerie, spike-heeled slippers, nail and hair appointments, and what would happen later Valentine's evening. The other four, including me, listened with great interest to something we had obviously never done.

It was surprising to the two Valentine enthusiasts that the rest of us didn't engage in the ritualistic dance of this commercial holiday. Yes, my husband always bought me a card, candy, and flowers, and I bought him a card and maybe a gift. But there was no overtone of exchange.

It was as if Valentine's Day was like registration renewal at the DMV. If you locked this day down, you were in and confirmed for another year. The way these women talked, they shared nothing else with their partners but sex, and their performance had to be stellar, replete with eye-popping garments to keep the charge cards, luxuries, and title of "Mrs." This conversation and the stress evident in their conversation awakened me to the emptiness between them and their husbands that must exist instead of a real, solid bond.

Was I stupid or naïve? The thought that I had to perform for my husband never crossed my mind. To be clear, our marriage was healthy and normal in every sense, but we enjoyed much more about each other than the physical relationship. Neither of us had to earn security in our marriage through emotional tricks or physical treats.

We laughed a lot. We talked a lot. We knew one another deeply. So much of my husband's appeal lay in his mind. He always had some obscure bit of information to share that I wouldn't have known otherwise. He taught me about opera, the stock market, international finance, and how to fight and win a battle. We fought many side by side and always emerged as the victors because we were a team. I was sure that nothing could divide us or come between us.

11

Hallowed Halls

For thirty years, I made a substantial investment in the life I shared with Eric in part because of my admiration and love and respect for my husband in particular and because of my desire to see a Black man rise. But Eric didn't rise alone, taking advantage of my investment and leaving me behind. No. He didn't take one step without holding onto my hand and pulling me upwards to walk side by side with him. Ours was a union of equals. We based our relationship on full equality, and Eric was never intimidated by my intelligence. In fact, he counted on it. My husband's unfailing response to any of my professional pursuits was, "Go for it, T! I got your back. Don't take no for an answer. We can do it together!"

He actually is the sole reason I have a doctorate from Columbia University. One day, while taking me for a ride, he stopped at Columbia, where he walked me through the halls of the revered university and through its campus. He suggested that I should apply for an advanced degree.

"Only smart people go here, and they would never let me in," I said.

Yet months later, he was sitting in one of the buildings on campus and helping me fill out an application and student loan forms. Somehow, he had convinced me that I should apply and assured me that I would indeed get in. That May, a letter came from admissions saying that I was admitted for the fall session.

I called Eric to say that I had something to show him but that he couldn't tell anyone.

"I got in! I got into Columbia!"

"Of course you did!" I could hear the smile in his voice.

"But please don't tell anyone. I don't want anyone else to know yet."

Keeping this milestone a secret was something he totally understood because we came from similar situations. As I was the first person on both sides of my family to graduate from college, my pursuit of advanced degrees was a notion that my elders wouldn't easily process. They might see it as unnecessary, or even evidence of pride. So my advancement should remain a secret for the time being, especially from my family.

My years at Columbia in the 1980s were not all hallowed halls and vast libraries. This time brought unwanted advances and an inappropriate incident of touching in a faculty member's office, changes in my doctoral advisor due to the admittance of my professor into the hospital to "dry out," and laughter at my dissertation defense in response to my saying, "My future goal is to work here with you all."

For many years, I didn't understand the laughter. But several years and numerous attempts to come back to my alma mater and work there opened my eyes wider and wider each time I didn't get the job opportunity or letters of recommendation. In fact, I was so stressed out by my experience that I faithfully kept my grandmother's cross and my *Daily Word* on the desk in front of me as a reminder that someone dear had believed in me and that Someone powerful was on my side.

For all of the stress Columbia brought me, I received more than equivalent amounts of encouragement, support, and motivation from Eric. My husband was there every step of the way. If I came home telling him one of these stories of hardship or discrimination, his next words were, "We will fight it, T."

Confidence and support were his response to everything. His fighting spirit and track record of rising up against any and all adversity made me feel like I was safer and more protected than anyone in the world. I never doubted that any problem could be fixed because Eric's motto was, "No isn't an answer. It is only making you find the best route."

In the end, I not only obtained a master's degree in psychology from the City University of New York, Queens College, but I also earned a master's degree in management and a doctorate in administration from Columbia University, all before the age of thirty. Eric and I were a team through it all.

That time in my life brought other changes, too. The day I found out I was pregnant with my first child, I called Miss Francis and said, "I need you."

Miss Francis, who hails from Jamaica, had been in our family for a decade. We met her when my grandmother needed part-time care, and she became like a grand aunt to me. I had kept contact with her after the death of my grandmother two years prior, and I knew she would be the best person in the world to take care of my son.

Miss Francis was highly protective of my son. Every day when I left for work or to run errands, she and my son would stroll the blocks of expensive homes in Jamaica Estates, with "him," my two-year-old son, waddling back and forth and Miss Francis a step behind, twirling the house key on the end of a long rope.

Finally, the day came for my graduation from Columbia University!

"T," asked Miss Francis, "We dressing him up for the photo?" The photo would be of all of us before I headed out the door with my doctoral robe and cap on.

"Yes, thank you, Miss Francis," I replied.

"Him going to look so cute in his new outfit," Miss Francis replied.

The elevator opened to the lobby. It was early, and my family and I took up much of the space. My mother, father, sister, husband, and I, in my beautiful blue robe with black velvet stripes and my velvet hat, stepped out together. As I entered the lobby, the maintenance and front desk attendants applauded me. First tears. To my surprise, a long, black stretch limo had parked in front of the circular driveway, and the driver opened the door saying, "Hello, Dr. Williams." Second tears.

That day, rain poured on us like the sky would release every drop of rain it ever held.

"Good luck, all of this rain," said my father.

"Don't worry, Teresa," my mother said. "It will all be fine."

Most times, my mother would speak encouraging words to me in reference to my pursuits. I needed to hear those encouraging words that day, because I was feeling sadness and nervousness mixing with my excitement.

The limo stopped in front of Riverside Church, where the convocation began at 10 a.m. for my department. Another woman of color and I yelled our heads off as they announced our degree and department. The look we exchanged was clearly one of solidarity that spoke words beyond other students' comprehension.

Our eyes admitted the truth that we didn't acknowledge verbally, that we had come to this moment of triumph after a gut-wrenching journey. We had passed an exercise in endurance beyond the measure of our white peers as we pursued our doctorates. In fact, emotion overtook my fellow student. Adorned in her Muslim headdress, she loudly proclaimed her thanks to Allah for helping her to "fight the fight" through this institution. Being one of two women awarded doctoral degrees (mine in Education Administration and Management) that year in our department was incredible, exhausting, and exciting—all at once. Together, my classmate and I celebrated the culmination of a grueling and discriminatory experience. I knew exactly what she was shouting about.

Once it was time to move to the quad at Columbia, we found hundreds of empty seats because of the sheets of rain. My family waited in the limousine, but I headed to the quad. You could easily count the few people standing in the quad facing the podium with the president of Columbia University reading a very condensed statement.

I was standing next to another student in the soaking rain. We looked at each other and smiled. Both of us were drenched, and as the president said, "Move your tassels over," we hugged each other and said, "Congratulations." I never knew who that other student was, but I will never forget that moment.

All of a sudden, the rain stopped wetting me. I looked beside me to see my husband holding a giant umbrella over my head. He had planned our celebration lunch at the Columbia Club, and the family went there next. The view of the city from the club was unbelievable. It looked like a place for important scholars. I felt like one that day.

If there is one thing, maybe only one thing I can say changed my life forever, it was the day my husband brought me to Columbia University and said, "Apply." I have spent many years troubled by my lack of advancement in my profession, even with the doctorate from Columbia University. I still am discouraged by the difference between what I thought this degree would be and what it has been. But I'm sure that I needed the title of "Dr." before my name in battles I had no idea I would face over and over again.

Looking beyond the troubles of my last married years and the questions I have, I can still say "Thank you" to Eric for taking me under his wings and seeing the potential in me. *Thank you. For this, I'm forever grateful.*

After graduation from Columbia University, I

went to work for a local Black newspaper.

After leaving the Board of Education and managing a citywide Black-owned newspaper for several years, I started my own publication. One day, I came home and said to Eric, "I want to start my own paper." My husband signed on to the idea of my starting *New York Trend* immediately. After all, we had started a business together before we were even married. So, he wrote the first checks for this new business.

Thirty years later, I continue to own *New York Trend* newspaper, still a highly respected and awarded publication cataloged in the Library of Congress, as well as the largest Black-owned newspaper in Long Island. *New York Trend* was my brainchild.

It was a great time. I was a new mother. My husband was doing well on Wall Street. We lived in the most exclusive luxury building in Queens, and I loved my life. On one family trip with our children, we visited The Library of Congress and saw *New York Trend* on display. To see something that had begun as a dream now forming a part of history was a great moment.

When Eric and I left the building, we looked at each other and turned away at the same time so that the kids wouldn't see us both crying simultaneously.

12

Moving on Up... The American Dream

One weekend, Eric was driving by the neighborhood temple when he saw a sign advertising an art fair the following weekend. He called me excited.

"T, next weekend is the Temple Art Show. Write it down on your calendar. Okay?"

The call didn't surprise me. We loved to shop antique fairs, and my husband had a great eye for art. So, the next weekend, we went to the neighborhood temple art show. As we drove there, I could see his anticipation and remarked on it.

"You are really excited to get there?"

"I'm hoping to get some Hebrew artifacts."

I understood. I knew that my husband's mother had been White from a prominent Jewish family. A piece of Jewish art would be deeply personal for him.

When we arrived, Eric said, "This is great, T. Look at all of this art and these sculptures!"

We spent at least two hours there browsing, and he was mesmerized by the historical pieces in the show. We wandered around until he saw one piece.

"T, look at this! The details and the symbols on this piece.

I agreed, it was a unique piece, the first piece of art my husband and I would purchase together. It was a sculpture of a unicorn made of gold with religious symbols etched into it that represented the Jewish faith. The weight of the horse was surprising. It was a very heavy, solid metal object. This golden horse was the first of many pieces of art we would collect carefully.

I now have the horse in my home in a special place. It has traveled to each of my homes and will always be a special reminder of the happy times in our union. When we first brought it home, we placed it on a shelf in our new cooperative apartment in one of the most exclusive luxury buildings in Queens, which was very different from our first apartment.

When we first married, I moved into his studio apartment in a building that was in transition. Mice and inhuman-sized roaches lived amongst us. Although the neighborhood was costly, the building was a blight on the surrounding properties.

On our weekend walks through the neighborhood, Eric and I would talk about our plans, hopes, and dreams while we house-shopped. We very quickly found a one-bedroom apartment further down the block. The building where we wanted to move was beautiful. Its huge apartments boasted high ceilings and prewar structure. The building was home to White middle-class residents. There were no Blacks in any of the surrounding buildings, either.

On one occasion, we met the superintendent of the building and asked about availability. He directed us to the management office, where we filled out an application for a one-bedroom apartment. My husband was relentless and called every week about openings in the building.

One year later, as we watched moving vans pull up and move residents in and out, we began to think we were being ignored.

A young Black woman finally gave my husband a definitive analysis of our situation. One day, when he called, she said, "I can talk today. When you and your wife came in to fill out an application, I wanted to tell you then that you would never be called. There are no Black people in the buildings managed by this office."

My husband thanked her for her candor. But the next thing I knew, Eric and I had an apartment in that very building. He later gave me the details. He said that he called the manager and promised to bring our situation to the NAACP, the Urban League, and Reverend Al Sharpton. He intimated that protesters carrying signs about discrimination would gather in front of every building the company managed. Evidently, the owner of the management company and the buildings, the real estate mogul father of Donald Trump, saw that discrimination wasn't good for business.

An easy transition? No. But my husband and I were mavericks in this area. We were a young couple chartering new territory, and we wanted to live accordingly.

Though we lived in that building for two years, our sights were set higher, right across the street. We would sit outside and watch the residents of the building pull up into the circular driveway and drop items off. At times, a maintenance person would bring out the shopping cart just at the beep of a horn and unload the car. The lobby had a huge chandelier, which was beautiful at night. The nicest cars went down the ramp and into the underground parking garage.

My husband and I wanted to live there, and when Eric went to work on Wall Street, our dream came true. We bought our first property, a one-bedroom with a terrace. It was an amazing time. We were excited about our lives and future.

Not only did we "move on up" in our address,

but my husband moved into finance. The transition from educator to Wall Street maven was easier for him because I supported the change. At that time, though what I could earn was very limited, I provided the financial means for our daily living expenses. It was very clear that Eric needed to be able to pursue his dreams in finance and feel confident in taking this step. The decision resulted in him becoming a successful financial leader.

We lived in that third building for ten years. When we moved out, my husband was a Wall Street vice president, and I owned and managed my newspaper. We followed the moving van across the Queens border into Long Island and pulled up in front of a bigger high-rise with acres of land on a golf course. We had really earned that nickname of "The Jeffersons" that my father had coined. I felt that we had made it. We had moved up.

Ten additional years passed, and the need for more space to accommodate our family brought us to a unique home where we settled for almost two decades. The home was inside a converted mansion with trey ceilings, hardwood floors, brick walls, and the detailed design of a 1920s mansion in a gated community.

We had a plan, and we worked the plan. Success was a team effort. We made wise investments and real estate decisions. My husband would say that a man should make twice as much as his father to be considered a success and to elevate the next generation. We went far beyond that measurement in economic, academic, and professional achievements.

In 2007, all signs were pointing towards a crisis in our economy. But I wasn't too worried. I watched my husband navigate our three-decade union through many crises, and we always landed on our feet. The expenses of our upper-middle-class life mirrored a marriage that was based on mutual respect, support, designated roles, and a common goal. We surpassed our parents' financial and educational status by leaps and bounds. We measured our success against those around us: foreign cars, private schools, extensive travel, fine clothing, and a stellar home that we worked our asses off to acquire and maintain.

Many, many times, I thought that I was a real-life Black Cinderella living a life I had never before had the capacity to dream. In fact, I didn't dream as a little girl. Didn't know how.

My husband and I were like a well-oiled machine. What I missed, he caught, and vice versa. He was our team's coach and captain. Having been a star athlete throughout his academic career, my husband often referenced sports analogies in an endearing way. He often said, "We are a team that can't be beaten. You and I are like a well-oiled machine. We can tackle any problem together. We are the champions!" For him, our team was the winning team. Nothing could ever come against us to divide us. And for three decades, what he said was true.

13

Say My Name. Say My Name.

One of my husband's proudest moments was the day I graduated with my doctorate from Columbia University. He beamed with excitement at my achievement. The fact that I could be called "Dr." had fulfilled a dream that started for him with our first trip to the school.

He was so proud of me and this great achievement that he wanted me to tell the world who I was so that I could get the respect he felt I deserved. He didn't look at stating my degree to others as boasting. He recalled the stories I told him of being a little girl who was so shy that she could never look others in the eye, and so she walked with her head down. He now looked at this person who was once that shy girl holding a doctorate diploma in her hands, and he thought that she was as smart as the others at Columbia to have done it. So, he made it his mission to convince me to introduce myself as "Dr. Williams."

This request brought some contention into our relationship, because the shy girl came back while the doctor retreated. Changing my mind took some time, but in my quest to earn the respect of those around me, I learned that it was an advantage to say that I was Dr. Williams. So I gradually began to use my title more and more. I would need it soon.

Jamaica Estates had worn out its welcome with one unsettling incident. Coming out of the parking lot to enter The Camelot (a luxury high-rise cooperative with a doorman and terraces, which was our next step up after the Kensington), I was chased by a guy with a knife and barely made it to my door. This neighborhood, too, was changing and once again bringing danger to my stoop.

So Eric and I decided to leave Jamaica Estates. Nowhere was it more necessary to be Dr. Williams than when Eric and I moved to the North Shore of Long Island. In order to gain approval for the apartment we wanted, we went before the board within a very Jewish community—99% Jewish and 1% other.

After hearing the story of his heritage (a Russian-Jewish mother and Black father), the chairwoman loved Eric. He and the board members held a warm and lively conversation. As the meeting wrapped without the board having asked one question of me, the chairwoman, looking only at my husband, said, "You know what? You are going to be very happy here, very happy."

Walking out, I mimicked her.

"What about me? Am I going to be very happy here, very happy?"

Eric looked at me, smiled, and said.

"Don't worry, T. You're with me."

Moving to the North Shore was not as wonderful as my husband thought it would be. He worked long hours on Wall Street. Longer work hours and a longer commute meant that we lost some of the hours we normally shared in the evening. But in exchange for the shorter commute, we enjoyed the gated community in an apartment that overlooked the Manhattan skyline, Connecticut, and the Long Island Sound. What was not to love?

Still, weeks before we were ready to move in, I prayed that the cooperative board wouldn't approve us. After the scrutiny of the co-op board and the comments to my husband about how he alone would be comfortable there, I felt that I wouldn't fit in. So often, due to his fairer appearance, my husband was accepted more readily than I. And I feared to forfeit the comfort of my present home to try this new environment, no matter how much safer and more prestigious it was.

At the time we moved, the integration into this area that was high-end to wealthy to "more money than God" had been almost non-existent. In our complex of three high-rise buildings with approximately 5,000 residents, I discovered only four Black homeowners. I saw even fewer in the toney shopping strip of the Miracle Mile, home of the Americana Mall, to which Rodeo Drive takes second place.

I weathered insults and imposing questions. Two stand out so clearly to me. Due to our packed schedules, I needed to hire someone to clean the apartment every other week. As the doorman suggested, I posted a card on the bulletin board, hoping to get someone who already worked in the building. But until that day, I was back to my ammonia and Clorox days with my hair tied up, scrubbing, mopping, wiping, and vacuuming all by myself. My grandmother would have been proud that I paid attention during those Saturday and summer lessons in keeping house.

On one of these days, the doorbell rang. I opened it to find a woman standing and smiling in the hall.

"Hi," I said. "Can I help you?"

"Yes," she replied with a heavy Slavic accent. She set one foot in the apartment and stuck her head in further, looking from left to right. Then she asked, "When will the lady of the house be home? I see on the board downstairs she is looking for cleaning woman."

"She's here," I replied.

"Then get her!" the woman said harshly.

I took a long, long, deep breath, and with a smile said, "She's here. Right here. In front of you. I'm looking for the cleaning woman. I'm the lady of the house."

We all know how this story ended. She turned blue with embarrassment. I thanked her politely, shut the door, and cursed the shit out of her to myself. Note to self—*I have got to stop cursing alone.*

The second of many painful incidents of racial discrimination involved my car. Eric felt that cars were markers of success. One of the first things he did when we moved to the North Shore was to make a trip to Rallye Motors, where he bought me a Mercedes Benz.

"I want you to feel confident wherever you go out here. I want people to respect you and know to stay off your ass," he said strongly.

So I drove around in a Benz, and I got looks of surprise and looks of disdain. A truck driver, who must have felt that I shouldn't be behind the wheel of a high-end luxury car, spat on me. Needless to say, I also increased the work for the Nassau County Police Department, who regularly followed and questioned me.

Driving While Black (DWB)—that was me! Being so blessed to drive a Mercedes Benz was not pleasant for me at all on the North Shore. In fact, I always had company that I didn't invite. Cops constantly stayed on my back, tailgating me so closely that I could see their eyes in my rearview mirror.

One night while I was driving home in the dark, I looked in the rearview mirror to exit the interstate, and damn! There were two eyes—so close that they seemed like they were sitting in my back seat. No lights flashed on top of the car. Those eyes could have belonged to anyone: a rapist, a murderer, or a thief. I didn't feel much safer than I had running from that knife-wielding maniac back in Jamaica Estates. Those eyes followed me in an unmarked black police car off the exit and then pulled up alongside me, laughing, and sped off.

I endured too many of the DWB incidents to recall. Just suffice it to say that I kept the police busy. Judging from the face of that one nighttime police stalker from the exit ramp, I also kept them amused.

Besides driving, I suffered other demeaning incidents. One shopping day turned out to be another lesson in racism. I was enjoying a stroll at the Americana Mall, window shopping, and I left to get into my car. Walking towards the car was an expensively dressed elderly woman. She came over to me with a bright smile.

"It's so nice that your lady lets you drive her car. I let my girl drive sometimes, too!" I got into the car and cursed the shit out of her to myself. Note to self—*I have got to stop cursing with no one to hear.*

Housing discrimination was another issue. As I knew, our home-buying agenda never had an end. As we made more, we invested more and sought to improve the level of our housing. One of our favorite ways to pass the time was to buy a home magazine and visit open houses on the weekends. Afterward, we would have dinner and wine and go over what we had seen that day. We would talk of our big dream home and future goals. Corny? Maybe. That was who we were.

But I found that we were not having the same experiences during these visits to the model homes and open house events. My very fair-skinned, mixed-raced husband got to roam freely like the other visitors to the open house. Me? I had a body on my heels from the time I entered until I left. So, I changed my strategy. I stayed with my husband and left with my husband. I had realized that some people didn't like us, but I hadn't known that some of them hated us—or at least me.

While the police followed me for being Black, the working class assumed that I didn't belong because I was Black and the insanely wealthy thought I couldn't be anything more than a servant because I was Black, I thought back to the neighbors planting tulips and pulling weeds on my childhood block. I thought of how I had wanted to be happy like them. But I could never be happy *exactly* like the women on my block. First, they were White. Second, they were White, and third, they were White women.

I'd have to find my own way to be happy. I'd have to find a way to get the world to see me for who I was. And I would have to find a way to get the world to say my name. The one I'd earned.

14

My Warrior Falls

In 2007, I turned fifty. That year, I could sense that something around me was getting ready to spin out of control. Eric threw me a 50th birthday celebration. Looking back, it seems that my party was the last good time we had. But I was not happy at that party. I was unhappy because he had told me earlier in the month that he had begun a new business venture that would take him away on weekends. Weekends were *our* time.

Beginning this new business was the first time that he had done something without consulting me and including me. My instinct was telling me that something was going wrong. Eric had flown my brother in for my party, and when I saw him, I fell into his arms and cried. I knew that something was going on, but I never suspected that the wrongness would crumble and destroy every aspect of life as we had known it.

From the end of 2006 through 2009, the housing market tanked, and Wall Street wobbled and hobbled until it crashed. Stockbrokers like my husband were facing the abyss. As was always his method, my husband had seen this financial debacle coming and expanded his business into foreign countries. This expansion was part of what had brought that drastic change to our lifestyle, what made him travel a lot, and what unraveled our pattern of togetherness.

Along with this travel came new associates. I later found out that they were not family men with wives and children. Eric became associated with men who enjoyed *Carnival* in Trinidad and one-night stands. The changes in him and in our relationship started right after his new venture with the new associates, whom I didn't particularly like. The change was a gradual one. Eric was no longer the doting husband, the committed family man. He was becoming snappy.

Again, I chalked that change up to life stressors like his growing responsibilities at home, his new business venture, and his becoming middle-aged.

My husband and I at one point even spoke to a therapist. I remember the therapist asking me in front of him, "What is one thing you are sure about in your marriage?"

I unequivocally and immediately answered, "That my husband would never step out on me." In my mind, Eric and I were best friends. If things came to the point of danger in our marriage, he would talk things out with me.

So, no, I didn't listen to that feeling that something was wrong. I couldn't. Any signs I might have noticed were like crop circles to me—unbelievable and ultimately explained with logic.

I can't tell you the exact day or time that my husband got into bed with another woman, but I do know that after one of his trips, he came home with a new haircut. Cutting his hair was *my* job. It was *our* special activity. Sunday nights, we spent talking about the forthcoming week. He read *Barron's,* the financial newspaper, while we listened to soft music, and I would trim his hair. In fact, I was the *only* one that had cut his hair since we had met. And the fact that he had allowed another woman to touch his hair should have told me to open my eyes and see *There's a woman after your man.*

People ask me all the time if there were any signs. Any signs my husband would lead a double life? Yes, looking back, I can see that there were signs. But in my mind, what was going on at home would never have added up to an affair. From all I could see— all I knew after thirty years of talking and sharing and knowing—was that Eric was stressed and going through a personal crisis.

But one huge signal should have been the way he reacted when I was diagnosed with breast cancer. I remember the minute the call came. I could hear my doctor speaking in low tones. I looked at my husband, who showed no emotion, and I immediately started screaming, crying, and rolling on the floor. I took the phone, and all my doctor could say was "T," which was what those close to me called me with affection. All I said to him was, "I have no one. I have no one. I have no one anymore."

I ran to my husband, laid my head on his lap, clung to his knees, and grabbed tightly. I looked into his eyes.

"Why is this happening to us?"

"I don't know, T," he said as one solitary tear ran down his face.

Only one tear for his wife of twenty-eight years, the mother of his children, his longest-lasting, closest, and best friend? He shed that one tear, but he followed it with no embrace, no reassuring words, no hugs, kisses, or any confirmation that "We will get through this," or "I love you," or "We will make it," or "You will be fine."

He never spoke those words. He just sat. Mr. Magic wasn't there anymore.

On Friday morning of Memorial Day weekend in 2009, my husband woke up early. He was reluctantly getting up because he was scheduled for a business trip out of state for the holiday weekend. He was going with his new business partner, the woman who turned out to be *that* woman. But I was still clueless at the moment.

"Why do you have to go?" I asked. "No one is doing business this weekend."

"I have to go."

"Let her handle whatever it is, and you cancel," I pleaded.

"Can't," he replied with an exhausted voice,

Before he left, he gave me a kiss goodbye. I followed him to the front door.

"I think you need a jacket."

"No, I'm fine." I shut the door.

Seconds later, I heard the door open.

"T," he called out. "Getting a jacket."

I rushed back to the door. As he left, I watched him walk towards the outer door. The glass door shut. In that second of exiting, he turned around and stopped, held onto the doorknob as if he wanted to come back in. Then he turned around and walked toward the waiting town car. Those moments of sadness and hesitation were our last minutes together.

Our regular driver saw me months after my husband died. He said that the two of them talked as usual on the way to the airport.

"He said he didn't want to go. He wanted to stay at home," the driver told me.

I wish he had.

May 30, 2009, marked the tragic and untimely death of my hero, my best friend, my loving husband, my knight in shining armor, and my Mr. Magic Man, who made all my dreams come true. He died away from me and cheated me out of the chance to try to save him from sudden death.

That cloudy, lazy Saturday afternoon was cool and breezy. I spent the morning leisurely working on a project at a friend's home. Part of the irony of that day and the weeks that led up to the very afternoon of my husband's death was that, somehow, my husband had brought me back to this safe haven of friendship, love, and protection right before he died.

It had been over a year since my husband and I had sat down with this couple, talked, eaten, had drinks together, and shared information about our businesses from the trials and tribulations to the excitement happening in our lives. We just clicked, even though this couple was at least a decade older and more experienced. But the difference was what made it good. They were still providing a learning experience for us.

My husband and I, like this couple, were partners, soulmates, and best friends who were intertwined and joined at the hip, even finishing each other's thoughts in our minds if not out loud. In them, I saw us, and I looked forward to decades more of feeling that I had all I needed in the world. I trusted my husband to prevent me from ever being lonely, afraid, or uncertain in this life. I trusted our love to live forever.

How does love die?

After Eric's death, his infidelities forced me to answer that age-old question.

Love dies when you get a phone call early on a Saturday afternoon, and a woman on the other end of the phone is crying and telling you that your husband is lying on a floor.

She had taken his phone to find my number, and she had called me. And then she handed the phone to a medic. The medic said that the paramedics were working on Eric. I kept shouting to the medic to tell me the second he was breathing. I kept holding on for what seemed like hours, collapsed in the middle of the street outside my friend's home.

That's how love begins to die.

Love was dying as my husband was, and then love was dead as the medic told me, "I am sorry, his heart is flat, and we are calling the morgue." The medic waited for my sobs to quiet.

"Who are you?" he asked.

"I'm his wife."

"Then who is *she?*"

If I could look back at past events through new eyes, changing the pattern of events to the way they should have been, I would go back to the day my husband died.

Instead of getting a harrowing phone call from a woman on the other end of the line, who turned out to be the root of betrayal, I would have awakened to my husband saying that he didn't feel well. I would have rushed around the bed, looked into his eyes, and asked him what was wrong. As I held his hand, soothing his fears with my reassuring words that all would be well, I would have called 911 on the phone right by the side of our bed.

He would have asked for some water and for some help from me to get him to his favorite big chair in the bedroom, only steps away from the bed. I would have put his comfy UGG slippers on his feet.

To keep us both calm, I would have brought up a funny story we both knew as I dressed to ride to the hospital with him if it became necessary.

I would have taken my rightful place by his side as he complained of chest pain and held my hand tightly. I would have rubbed his head, running my hands through his hair, and saying, "You need a trim." Kneeling down, I would have laid my head on his shoulder and given him a hug.

He would have heard my screams, not hers, as he looked at me one last time. Slowly keeling over in his favorite chair, he would have felt me trying to hold him up until he finally lost consciousness.

If I could look back through new eyes, I would have laid my head on his chest and held him one last time. I would have been the one dealing with the EMS workers. I would have stayed right beside my husband as they fought to bring him back. I would have watched the funeral directors place his body into the plastic bag, and I would have walked beside that body to the hearse.

Why was I not there? My rightful place was beside him. Not hers. She didn't have the right to watch my Mr. Magic, my warrior, my best friend, die! She hadn't earned that right through thirty years of loyalty.

But she thought she deserved my place and more. That's why she and her mother contacted my husband's secretary. That's why they tried to discover the funeral service details. Luckily for me, my brother was aware of their intent and alerted the ushers, sharing their descriptions in order to keep them from attending. I would later find this out and more.

If I could look at this day through new ideas and change the details, I would see the day my husband died without the stench of betrayal. On that day, the universe would say, "Job well done" to a man who lived to be a friend to all, a protector, a father, a successful international businessman, a wonderful husband, a great brother-in-law, and a thoughtful son-in-law, not the victim of his need to prove his virility with a worthless accomplice.

We had promised each other to remain faithful until death parted us. But my husband parted from me before death took him. He should have shared the hour of his death with me. The good girl. The good wife.

Part III
The Strong Woman

No More Nerve Endings

I have a very good friend whom I have known since we were in first grade. Recently, she asked me to edit and review a proposal for her. I was glad to do it. Her response to my work was, "Now I know why I came to you! This is unbelievable, and you did it in no time."

I wrote back to her, "Thank you for asking. Your response has given me a needed boost to my confidence that I can do something well. "

My friend responded, "What has life done to you to have hurt your confidence, Who has taken away your power? You are amazing."

My answer? "Life."

This discussion had me thinking. Where is our strength? What does it come from? What do we seek when we need to recharge? Who do we turn to when we need to hear, 'It's going to be okay"?

For me, it was my best friend and partner in life. My husband. Some might ask if my answer should have been 'God.' Well, I believe that God brought my husband and me together. I believed that God had blessed our union. I believed that we shared faith and spirituality as friends and lovers. So, in the vein of being a wife who saw the extra strength of a good man in her husband, I had faith in my husband's words, 'Everything will be OK. We will do this together. You and me.'

And never did a doubt cross my mind.

His death took so much out of me and away from me. I got even sicker. I had already been diagnosed with cancer. Fighting a deadly illness changes you forever. It wakes you up and says that you could die. Now. It tells you that no matter how tough, determined, or strong you think you are, there is something in your body that's trying to take you away. You are not invincible.

So when I think of the answer that 'Life' has done this to me, I think of no longer having my partner, who was a warrior, afraid of nothing, my safety net and my safe haven, my friend not there to hold my hand as devastating chemicals were poured into my body to fight the disease, or to wrap his arms around me as I sat on my sofa looking at my burnt fingernails and toenails, and he not there to let me lay on his lap as I cried.

'Life.' It has taken a light out of my soul that I try to relight. I overheard a friend talking about me to another saying, 'I see her trying to pull herself out of this, but she just can't.' And for a while, I thought she was right.

My critics might say that I expected too much from the man I called my husband and my friend. Or maybe I was weaker than I thought because I shouldn't have depended on him so much. My critics might say that I gave and trusted too much and that this is the expected result. But I would say to anyone that if you cannot admit to yourself that the world and life is a scary journey and it's made a little bit safer, kinder, tolerable, enjoyable, happier, sharing this journey, then you have not met your soul mate, the keeper of your heart.

So one day, recently, I mentioned to my closest confidante about my legal and financial matters—that I was facing a longer and threatening legal battle. He asked me, "How do you feel?" I responded, "I feel nothing. I am numb." He always makes me laugh about my troubles and responded, "You are like those people who break a bone and don't know it. You have no nerve endings."

I laughed hysterically and said, "That is the most perfect observation anyone has made about me." Except for matters of health and well-being of myself, my family, and my children, I challenge anyone to disturb the place of nothingness I occupy right now. The nerve endings are dead.

15

One Man, Two Lives

Before the storm broke that had been brewing as I turned fifty, I thought that in years to come, Eric and I would hold hands and enjoy the fruits of our labor: three beautiful, educated, brilliant children, a beautiful home, and a successful business. I thought we would be able to share our weekends taking our treasured drives, touring homes, stopping on the road in little inns for lunch, and seeing the world. Instead, I was left to celebrate death. His sudden death.

The bleak surprise celebration arrived one Sunday shortly after the untimely death of my love. It came in a letter from a government agency informing me that the social security payments being sent to my daughters would be reduced due to another child. *Shock. Beyond shock. Beyond disbelief.* I think my mind literally went numb. I know my heart stopped for a few seconds.

This letter is how I found out that my love, my love, was living a double life. This is how I found out that I had been betrayed. This is how I faced the fact that our oath that no one comes between us was dishonored.

I grabbed my keys and ran out the front door. I got into my car and drove, speeding on the highway, screaming, crying, and driving to nowhere. And as I drove and screamed and cried, I was filled with rage at the woman who continued to steal from me and mine.

But cursing that woman didn't erase the pain inside me. How could I reconcile the news in that letter with the life I had lived for thirty years? The caring and nurturing qualities of my husband, who was always trying to help me reach and set higher goals, still lived deep in my heart. Unfortunately, with the same zest and determination that he did what was good, he had inflicted pain, destruction, and mental torture on me and our children.

He had said that I was his whole life, and he treated me like his Empress for thirty years. My father had called us "The Jeffersons." We came from the neighborhood, then we slowly but steadily moved on up and up and up. *Together.* I couldn't excuse or forgive him, but what could a man do when pussy was thrown in his face, sitting on his face, riding his penis, and humping him apple style?

I don't know, but it must be tough to turn down no matter how much you love your wife and your home and your children and your life. It must be like when you are bitten by a venomous snake and will be paralyzed within hours if an anecdote isn't given. Well, there was no anecdote given, and my husband succumbed to the venom of the nastiest kind of snake bite—a fatal bite mixed with a little cocktail of bewitchment dropped in a glass while his back was turned.

I started to fight back the second I realized that my children and I were under siege.

Those individuals who had gotten close to my late husband were not satisfied with the monetary rewards of their association with him. More specifically, *That Woman* who laid down with my husband took steps to extort money out of me and befriend my children by contacting them through social media.

I had to battle these attempts.

That Woman claimed that she had produced a child with my husband, and for weeks I would receive phone calls late at night. When I picked up the phone, I could hear baby sounds and the sounds of baby toys, and then the caller would hang up. These calls made me feel like a victim. Powerless. They exacerbated my husband's betrayal, the fact that he would even bring me into an association with such an individual. I received letters from attorneys with false information that threatened my standing as the executor of my husband's estate. All were futile attempts either to drive me insane or to get money that was not deserved.

This chapter is a very hard one for me to write because the wounds and hurt of the past still affect my life every day. I was taught that to sin was to go against the doctrine of Christianity. I was raised in a household of strong Christian values and ethics. There was no middle ground in my home. Things were either black or white, right or wrong, and any attempts to explain away behavior that couldn't be defined as such were deemed futile. Lying was a sin in my home. If you were a liar, then you were also considered a thief, and if you were a thief, then you could easily become a murderer. And it turned out that the man I married and loved with all my heart had committed this sin and more.

If I could now ask him what happened, I would begin by asking why he betrayed me and our children. I would ask him about the love of people we shared, and at the top of the list would be our grandmothers, whom we loved and adored so much. I had never met his grandmother because she had passed away before our friendship, but my husband loved, honored, and cared for my own as if she were his grandmother, too.

I will never know the depths of despair that caused his betrayal of all who loved him so much. After his death, I cleaned out his wallet. My grandmother, in her last days, had been hospitalized, and he had sent her a huge floral bouquet with a card that read, *Katin, please get well soon so I can eat again.*

The Sunday morning that my grandmother died, he came to the hospital with me before the staff moved her body. On the side of her bed was the pink vase full of fresh flowers and the card he had written. When we left, I took the vase, which now sits on my dresser. Unknown to me at the time, he had taken the card. My grandmother died March 17, 1985. My husband died May 30, 2009. He carried that little reminder of Katin until the day he died. It had still been in his wallet. It reminded him of Sunday best, our first shared dinner in my family home.

So now after all that has happened, I struggle to understand why he thought there was anything in his life we couldn't fix together. Months after his death, years after his death, and even today, I still ask myself if I missed something wrong. How could my very best friend find a reason to lie to me, to leave me out of his deepest troubles and thoughts, or to hide his pain?

What happened to make a man who loved me so deeply turn and join others in a conspiracy against me? This relationship with *That Woman* was not a one-night stand. And it became a calculated plan to destroy me in every way possible.

I have had to accept the fact that the man I loved and who shared my life was not just meeting the need for a sexual escapade. He had become a stranger to me who took on a co-conspirator to break down—coldly and systematically—a home, a family, a friendship, a team, a lifelong partnership.

I wanted answers to my questions. *Were you caught up in something and couldn't find your way out? Were you the victim of something that was powerful enough to make you desert your own family and watch them be destroyed? When did you become such an evil force? Did I miss something decades ago?*

One memory comes to my mind.

The singer Chaka Khan was my husband's favorite performer. One birthday, I blindfolded him and drove him to a small venue where she was performing. We had second-row seats. Ironically, as she came off stage and sang through the audience, she ended up coming over to him, sitting on his lap (with my permission), and singing her signature song, which was also "our" song, "Through the Fire." It was as if I had planned the whole night.

I think back now over the three decades we spent together and all the "fires" we suffered together, and I wonder how he could think that I wouldn't walk through any fire with him again.

I've gone through the gamut of whats and whys, explanations for unexplainable behavior like a severe mid-life crisis or a one-night stand gone wrong. I wish it could have been something so easily explainable. Maybe that would have been a speed bump in our relationship instead of the tsunami that destroyed my home and almost took my life.

16

Nightmares Replace Memories

The brain is an amazing organ. I've always known that. As a mental health professional, I've had a longstanding fascination with the human brain. The brain protects us and guides us. It is our conscience and our enemy. The seconds, minutes, days, nights, weeks, months, and years that I suffered torment, disappointment, depression, illness, and loss increased the imminent danger of my brain turning on me. So much tragedy happened all at once.

I found a lump in my breast. The doctor said cancer. I had that breast removed and rebuilt. Seven surgeries of rebuilding. My husband dropped dead. I buried my husband. I had my chemo. I heard I would lose my hair. I opened an envelope and found out that my husband betrayed me. I took the red devil in my arm—the chemo that incinerates you, blackens your nails, and takes away your taste. Today, I'm still fighting legal battles. I'm fighting financial battles. I'm still grieving. I'm still angry. I'm alone and afraid.

All in one month, the world crumbled. My family was broken. I was broken.

I sat as a new widow, days old in my grief, in front of a doctor I had known for decades. His children went to school with mine. As soon as I heard the dreaded words of my diagnosis, I thought of him. I buried my husband on Tuesday and showed up at chemo on Thursday.

Chemo teach is a session that you take in order to educate you about the process of chemotherapy. Participants in the conversation include the chemo nurse, a nurse practitioner, a social worker, and you. During the session, the other people in the meeting inform you about the severity of chemo and its effects. You find out what is going to happen to you internally and to your physical appearance, including weight, hair loss, and discoloration. You also receive a tour of the treatment room, equipped with TV, blankets, and reclining chairs.

I met the social worker. While she talked to me, I saw her mouth moving. However, I heard nothing except my sister speaking into my ear, saying, "Speak! Answer!" I couldn't get words to come out of my mouth.

I was then led into the briefing room with the social worker, a nurse, and the instructor. The social worker handed me a kit. Inside a plastic bag was beige makeup, an eyebrow pencil, and a scarf.

I gave the bag back and said decidedly, "I won't need it. I'm not doing chemo."

I could hear my sister crying. I turned and saw her tears. She never cries. Never. She was begging me, "Please!"

Every plea of hers I met with the firm answer, "No. I can't and won't do it. I can't," I said. "Not without him. I can't do this. I'm leaving." That was how much I depended on and trusted my husband, strangely enough, even still.

As we all exited the room, one person stayed behind with me. It was the nurse. She touched my arm and asked if she could speak to me. We went back into the room alone. Of the many things she said to me, the last thing was, "Let's make an agreement. I can see beyond this time in your life. I don't know you, but God is telling me that one day, you are going to be on a book tour telling the world your story. God has brought us together for a reason. I don't know what it is, but if you will come to chemo, I will be here with you for every session."

I did go to chemo, as she predicted. And she kept

her promise. After I made the decision to attend chemo, she came to every session.

The weeks ahead were torturous. A number of enemies came after me. I was fighting a battle for my life while fighting against creditors, outsiders, and those businesspeople who were the residue of the last years of my husband's life. I'm sure that these vultures, whose identities were revealed to me in my illness, counted on me losing the battle for my life so that they could take what they thought belonged to them. Some people find joy and fulfillment in taking what they didn't earn, watching success turn to failure, and stealing another woman's man.

Every day for six months, I was either crying, battling my enemies, or praying while the invasive chemicals stripped me of beauty, weight, and strength. I feel as though I was the one living the double life. Everything in my life was overwhelmingly sad.

I had cancer and was enduring chemo. My husband had just died. I had discovered that my partner, my love, had betrayed me. On top of this, I was in a legal battle to keep what was mine and to protect my kids financially, something my financially smart husband had shockingly failed to do properly.

It was really all too much. By day, I put on a face of strength and determination and summoned the energy to meet my responsibilities for my children and myself. By night, I celebrated the dark and the end of the day. I prayed each night that it would be my last.

Night after night, I felt that God betrayed me. He didn't listen, no matter how hard I prayed. Every day when I woke up, I cursed Him for not taking me in my sleep. This pain, both mental and physical, had to stop.

I was so sad and distressed that my legs felt like weights. I struggled to take every single step. However, I figured out that once every legal detail was done, I wouldn't have a reason to stay alive. I could leave. I could leave my family secure. I would wait out the legal battles. I reviewed my will to ensure that it was airtight. I left notes about my safety deposit box, keys, etc. And I was well-equipped. I was ready to go.

One of the worst sides of our healthcare system is the absence of prescription monitoring. The amount of OxyContin I had been given easily would have knocked out a tribe of elephants. Every night, I would go to my bathroom, take out a bottle, and hide it behind the lamp on my nightstand.

Holding the bottle in my hand, I would say, "Once the legal issues are wrapped up, I can be gone." Then I would put the bottle on my nightstand, cap side up. In the morning, I would turn the cap side down. Yet another night, I would have to wait. For me, daylight meant that God hadn't taken me in the night. It was another day I would have to face.

I never actually said the "s" word to myself or anyone, but in my darkest moments for months after Eric's death, phone calls from friends constantly intruded upon me. I didn't know that my closest friends and those who I didn't even know cared so much for me made a calling circle. They would ask, "Where are you? What are you doing?" Then, someone would call to see if I had gotten out of the bed or left the house. I know I should have been appreciative, but honestly, at the time, their monitoring was so annoying. Why couldn't everyone leave me alone? Couldn't they just stop caring? I had stopped.

People ask, "How can people end their lives?" It's not about life. It's about the enemy who also lives in our brains and begs us to stop the pain.

I was not afraid of dying. I had seen heaven. The week before my chemo treatment, I got a tour of the facility, which included a room I can only describe as heavenly. I entered a huge white room where the lights were off. It was silent. Outside, a late cloudy afternoon filled the window. Inside the room, I saw white shades, white chairs, and a white floor. I glanced across the room, and there in a white recliner, wrapped in a white blanket, was a woman. She was motionless. A gurney beside her held tubes leading to her body. Her head was wrapped in a scarf. If this was like heaven, then I knew where I was going.

The nightmares I had were dreams in which I was alive. The memories of anything happy or good had been erased from my mind. Mr. Magic was gone from my memories. Smiling faces were gone from my dreams. No matter how hard I tried, I couldn't invoke one memory of my life before the devastation.

17

Drowning

Throughout August 2010, I was still waiting for the other shoe to fall. It was so hot every morning. This wig on my head stopped all the air that used to blow my hair in the breeze.

When I was a young girl, some of the same kids who called me names also called me Pocahontas. I had long, straight, black, Native American-like hair with a bit of curl. A year of cancer treatment stole it. I couldn't face the mirror every time I had to endure the gluing and ungluing ritual of my lace-front wig.

It was almost as painful as looking down at where

my full, 36DD, right breast used to dangle. I could see it, feel it, and enjoy the pleasuring of it by my husband. I didn't know why I was here anymore. I had been ravaged by chemotherapy, stripped of my hair, blackened my fingernails and toenails, burnt, deformed, and battered by betrayal. The pain was unbearable.

Pain didn't riddle my body as I had expected. The seven months of treatment were gracious to me. I functioned normally—if normalcy meant dealing with a greater pain and loss with the sudden death of my husband.

I couldn't even mouth the word cancer, and to this day, I don't say it. I speak about "it" as if it were a passing occurrence that left indelible scars: track marks that will never ever fade.

Something came into my body. It tried to kill me. It hid from me over time, and then, when I was at my weakest point, it showed itself. But even though I was suffering and being abused. Even though I was fragile and to the point of near mental collapse, I found it. And as my doctor said, I saved my life.

At the time of my diagnosis, however, I had two threats against my life: the illness and my husband. I didn't know then that he was trying to do the job that the illness might have done. I didn't know then that he probably cheered with satisfaction that something else would do the job.

I had fought many times throughout my life,

and here I was fighting again. This time it was not a changing neighborhood, bullies, discrimination, or even the other woman. This time I was fighting cancer.

One night, not too long ago after all the horror had happened, I collapsed on the floor of my bedroom from fatigue and dehydration. It seemed like I had the flu, but I was so caught up in the daily drudgery, responsibility, and pain that ran through my veins that I thought my heated forehead was a hot flash. For weeks, I was dripping in sweat, walking with weak knees, and unable to eat. I had done the same thing many times before. I pushed myself to exhaustion to get my jobs done. But this time was different. On top of being sick, I was scared. And my fear was what had truly stopped me from getting medical help.

One of my daughters was home and discovered me lying on the bedroom floor. She helped me into bed and brought me water. All throughout the night, I wavered between calling 911 and lying in my sweat. In and out of sleep, I thought through the alternatives: *Stay home and wait to see what will happen to me, or call an ambulance to get an IV drip of fluids and fever-reducing medications.*

I chose to stay home even though I was barely able to walk upright. My sheets were drenched with sweat, and I couldn't get comfortable enough to sleep for long periods of time.

Every time I moved, I could hear the rustling of

the black, leaf-sized garbage bags I had placed under my head just in case I got sick.

Not many things scared me. But this night, I was scared. My fear was not about what I might have or if I would survive the vomiting and diarrhea. I was scared of sitting in the hospital alone, unhinged, un-attached, with no man beside me, with no man to tell the doctor about me, and with no man to say that he was here for me and that he wouldn't leave me alone.

Have you ever ridden in an ambulance alone? I imagined what it would be like to do so, speeding on the highway with sirens blaring. The seat for your man, your significant other, is empty. When asked, "Who brought you here?" my answer would be, "I came alone."

After twenty-seven years of marital bliss, career success, and an American Dream life, I was be-trayed. Betrayed by my body. Betrayed by my hus-band. Betrayed by life. Betrayed by my own heart. I seemed to be part of a secret society of women who had been betrayed and who were faced with shame, anger, embarrassment, and fear.

Don't stare. If you do, you will catch them in deep thought, eyes faced down and off to the side but fixated on nothing, and lids nearly closed. It's the look of deep-seated pain, betrayal, hurt, and de-spair. Women who have experienced the lies, pain, fear, and panic that are the result of the betrayal of the man they love, for whom they bore children, and with whom they grew up all have the same look in their eyes.

Look deep into their eyes, and you will see a dark tunnel that leads to a broken heart and empty soul. I've joined their ranks. It's the secret society of women scorned, and we all hide beneath our fear, a fear of saying that we have lost to an unworthy opponent, the one who is the cause of our walk of shame.

It happened to me. I stand up. I raise my hand. I shout out louder than anyone else every single day, as I will do for the rest of my life, that I have been betrayed, cheated on, conspired against, and defeated in a battle I had no idea I was fighting. The unworthy opponent was shrewd, ruthless, crude, and calculating, and she worked in tandem with a team of evil perpetrators.

How can you fight against an opponent who you can't see because your eyes are filled with trust? How can you suit up with the appropriate armor when you don't know dress protocol for fighting for your life? What can you do to stop a perpetrator who has slithered her way into the deepest part of your bond and infected a purity of friendship, love, and unity?

You can't.

The lessons I have learned from the tsunami that became my life were fraught with mistakes, misgivings, and misjudgments. I looked back at my life and asked, "Why was I so trusting, naïve, invested, kind, true, loving, tender, and committed to what I thought was life at its best with the best?" I woke up to pain, and I suffered daily through personal heartache beyond my ability to describe. I shuddered to think that my life would continue like this: continually facing the unknown without the strength I counted on to see me through every problem and never, ever to feel alone again like this.

18

The Power of the Boob

On December 3, 2010, I was making my third trip, and hopefully my last, to the surgical center for the reconstruction of my breast. I knew the routine, and the nurses were friendly. I was not entering a huge, cold hospital but a beautiful townhouse, stunningly furnished and regal.

There was something surreal about having cancer procedures in such a beautiful place. Coming to a mini-mansion to have my breast rebuilt step by step was like getting my life back step by step. Though some women opt not to go through breast reconstruction, I liked having breasts. I felt like a piece of me was missing, so I needed to get a piece of me back.

My doctor went through his routine, drawing with magic marker on my body to outline a map of what needed to be identified, tweaked, and moved. He had been with me from the first day, and I knew that he felt for me and for all the health issues I had suffered. He assured me that all would go well with my surgery. I reminded him of the promise he had made: to make me feel like a woman again.

"I will," he said. "Your story is so believable." "So sorry," I responded. Then it clicked with me. "So you saw the article?" I asked.

"I heard about it, but I didn't read it," he responded "Read it," I said.

But he answered, "I don't think I should. It's just too sad."

The article to which he was referring had appeared in a major New York City daily newspaper. The article read that my attorneys filed a lawsuit to fight for what was rightfully mine. Once news reporters saw the legal filing documents (which were public record) I didn't have much of a choice about doing the interview. My attorney informed me that a local paper had uncovered the lawsuit filing and was going to do a story with or without me. He recommended that I comply to set the story straight. This decision was a terribly hard one to make because I couldn't listen to my own story. So, telling my story drained me to exhaustion.

The interview was conducted at my attorney's office, where a reporter interviewed me about my husband's double life. A photographer came. He snapped photos as I spoke. After almost three hours of questioning, recalling memories, and crying, the interview was over. The reporter wished me well. The photographer, a tough-looking street photographer who had seen the best and worst of New Yorkers, had tears in his eyes, just like the reporter.

At the end, they wanted to take one last photo. I have looked at that photo many times over the years and have thought, How could that be me? I had a tear-stained face, tear-drenched shirt, and a horrible wig covering my hairless head, but at least I had two boobs. I never expected anything from the reporter and photographer, but what I received was an unexpected gesture of kindness, encouragement, and support.

The article came out a week later. It ended my life-long efforts to be a private person. It told the story of a professional woman who was the victim of her husband's deceit and infidelity. I received phone calls from supposed friends who commented, "I would never have expected to see you in that paper. If anything, not in *The Times.*" It seemed like open season on me, and the wolves were circling for more gossip and a front-row view to watch my life fall apart. I didn't think the article was worth it.

It made me happy that I hadn't entertained the

various media outlets that had pursued me for years to do a Lifetime or Discovery Channel movie. The article was necessary once I saw that she had been interviewed also. I couldn't let that go unchallenged.

I chose to shield my children from as much as I could until I filed the lawsuit. After the article, the world knew it all. My children had to face friends, teachers, and family who now read about the double life their father had been living for two years. My children, who are strong, faced this public intrusion into our private lives with reserves of strength and class that touched me. They adorned me with statements like, "We are proud of you... We are sorry… The motto in this house is, 'We fight to the end.'"

But at the doctor's office on this day, I was trying to put that public embarrassment behind me. I knew that this man, this doctor, had been blessed with God's hands. I knew also that his sensitivity had been a source of strength.

He said, "I remember that you said, 'Please give me my breast back one day.' I will never forget what you told me."

I told him, "Losing my hair was worse than losing my breast." He said, "I love your hair. It's coming back so nicely."

We had an ongoing dialogue about hair. He recommended hair plugs, and we laughed.

I lay there staring at the chair where I knew my husband would have been had it not been for the tragedy. He'd have his cap on, pulled down low, scrolling on his phone, and patting me. He would say, "T, where you want to eat after?"

Always thinking about a good meal and sharing it together had been our thing. For the third time, the chair was empty. I could see the shoes and legs belonging to the husband of the woman next to me. Just like last time, I turned on my side and fought to hold back the tears. But this time, I couldn't stop the stream.

The nurse and anesthesiologist walked in and said.

"Don't be afraid. You're going to be fine." The anesthesiologist patted me on the shoulder. It felt like my husband's hand.

"I wasn't scared," I said. "I just miss my husband so much, and most of all, right now." The time had come for me to be sedated, and I said, "Just knock me out."

When I woke up in the holding area, it was done. I finally had a full set of breasts that matched. The doctor's blessed hands had surgically guided me almost back to where I started.

Why did I feel like that? It must have been the drugs. I had been living with anxiety for the past two weeks, with fright in my stomach and throat. Worry. Worry over my life, my kids, their lives, the lawsuits, the IRS audits, my office, my health, my future, my loneliness, and my hurt. I kept wondering what was next. What shoe is going to drop next? At that moment, I felt like I was balanced. God blessed me with twos: eyes, arms, legs, and breasts. I had been out of balance for many, many months, but on the day of my surgery, I almost felt like myself. I felt like a woman again. Almost. Almost was better than not at all.

Was that the anesthesia talking? I hoped that I had come to a turning point, that I could once again feel whole. I hoped that the feeling in my body meant that my children and I would be whole again.

Do you know what it feels like not to feel whole? To have a part of your body that defines most of who you are as a woman lopped off, like when you chop up a chicken to fry? You enter the hospital with your breast, and you leave with it gone.

Now, it was not gone. After my reconstructive surgery, I felt myself again. I felt stronger again. Other women might disagree, but without my breast, I didn't feel whole. With it, I did.

Though it might sound strange, I felt at that moment that I was in full fighting form again.

When I was not physically whole, for some reason, I couldn't feel like I was fighting on an even keel against all that had come at me, including a woman who relished in the size of her breasts, putting them out there for all to see, including my husband. She told me how tight she wore her clothing (all the time). I even saw the mementos she sent to my husband: Playboy-type photos with her huge breasts draped over her arm, posing them for my husband's eyes.

I remember lying in the hospital bed and getting a text on the phone from this woman.

She texted me that I didn't deserve this. She said I was a good person. She said I would be ALRIGHT in all caps. She texted me this as I lay watching a morphine drip numb the pain from the surgery that removed my right breast.

I was not surprised to get the text. I had no idea who she really was to my husband at that time. I just said to myself, I wonder if he knew how illiterate she was. She wrote in all caps and couldn't spell. I only felt anger towards her, wondering why she was intruding into my world at the worst moment of my life. I didn't know.

Why was it that now that my breast was back, I had power again? You can't point at me and see my weaknesses. I had been a shy and reserved individual my entire life. I had let very few people in and kept most people out. I lived a private life. No one knew what I didn't tell them until the loss of my breast. Then, anyone who knew that I had lost my breast would know that I had been weakened by illness. I couldn't hide because this illness didn't let me hide. It put everything out there, from my hair falling out to my breast getting removed to my skin turning pale. Still, everyone said that I looked well and that it was hard to think that anything was wrong with me.

But inside, I knew that she knew. She sent me that message to let me know she knew that I was one-breasted, disfigured. In fact, I recall her telling my husband that I didn't have "serious" breast cancer but that she knew somebody who had the "real" one. I can't believe that he repeated that to me at one point. I can't believe that I was still blind, thinking they were just business partners at the time. Still, I wondered why he had discussed me and this intimate issue with her. A few weeks before he died, I told my husband in a way that was out of character for me, "What fucking medical school did she graduate from?" For now, I pushed the question to the back of my mind as I had other immediate worries.

I never cursed around my husband. I had class and character. I was reserved, and he liked that. He liked that I was professional and supportive, that I was trustworthy, faithful, fun, introspective, communicative, supportive, funny, reliable, and comforting. He even told me that I was the only one on this earth who he totally trusted with his life, even after she had gotten her way with him.

After my surgery, I sat in bed and watched a marathon of Fantasia For Real. I was pensive, thinking about how Fantasia was accused of breaking up a marriage. In one episode, the lawyer told her that if there was a legitimate marriage and if it could be proven that a relationship still existed between her boyfriend and his wife, Fantasia could be culpable in their divorce.

Well, only two people who have shared life, a bed, and a special journey know when that journey has ended. In my case, the journey between me and Mr. Magic hadn't ended. In fact, in our marriage, we had been through bumps in the road for more than 30 years, but we always survived, stuck together, and were victorious in all our fights.

But this time was different. The bump that I had sensed had been turning into a blockade was this skank. The skank who was texting me while I was recovering from breast removal surgery. The skank who texted me during my cancer treatment. She was working her way between us long before any trouble existed in our marriage. She caused the trouble.

So, what was this feeling that I had as I awoke from the anesthesia? I couldn't explain it, but I prayed that it wouldn't leave. I didn't want to go back to having that anxiety in my every swallow. I relished the feeling of near wholeness again because I had two breasts that matched.

I felt like I was actually coming back to me, whoever that was now, with so many things changed, lost, and with my world turned upside down. Somehow, I felt like I could now face the other woman eye-to-eye with strength, confidence, and pride because she had nothing on me. Isn't that ridiculous? Sometimes, equality and self-confidence come down to the most basic things in life.

Here, I was a successful entrepreneur, an Ivy League grad, and the recipient of numerous accolades and awards. However, in a battle for a man, everything came down to the outer self, not the inner. In the end, we revert to our animal needs. Why her over me? Better sex? Kinky sex? Bigger breasts? Bigger ass? Taller? Thinner? We were not in a debate competition. We were in a battle of the breasts.

Though I'm not going to toot my own horn, I have earned the right to say who I am. I'm a tall, beautiful, healthy, athletically built, intelligent, cultured, well-educated Black woman of mixed heritage with thirty years of exceptional accomplishments who has raised three exceptional adults. And, by the way, I have two breasts.

Again.

<h1 style="text-align:center">19</h1>

The Good Girl Has Died

One night in 2012, I was home alone because my girls were sleeping over at their friend's house. I lay in bed binge-watching one of my favorite comedy sitcoms, *Everybody Loves Raymond*. I had become even more addicted to shows with happy families because mine wasn't complete anymore. The warm stream of tears down my cheeks had become so familiar. At this point, I still didn't understand how I had gotten here. I believed that if misery, sadness, and despair ever had a child, it was me. I never imagined that life could have been as devastatingly cruel as it had been for the past three years.

I lay there talking to God and asking Him every single question about everything that had happened: one at a time. I then followed each question with a definitive statement of how I was praying for each one and a clear statement of how I was counting on a positive and successful outcome that would bring my children and me the victory. I'm sure that I also requested some retribution, even though I knew I wasn't supposed to ask for that. My prayers sounded something like this:

Dear God, I have worshiped you and believed in you from my first memory of my mother and me kneeling side-by-side reciting, 'Now I lay me down to sleep, I pray the Lord my soul to keep, If I should die before I wake, I pray the Lord my soul to take.' I have been a good girl, a good daughter, and a good wife. I raised my children to have faith and to believe in a higher power. Can I ask you, Lord? What did I do wrong? What did I do to have such pain and terror enter my life and destroy the life I knew?

But I'm still going to stand in faith and declare: 'My children and I will see the victory! I will win these battles! I will remain healthy! I will keep the faith and have no doubt that You, God, are in control! You fight my battles, Lord! I know You won't let evil win, and You will cause justice to prevail! Justice prevail, oh, Lord in Heaven! Hear my cries, Lord! Let justice prevail! Amen.

I prayed, shouting loudly.

"'Vengeance is Mine!' says the Lord."

But I can't help but want some revenge after the permanent physical scars of an illness, the deformity of my body for life, the sudden death of my husband, and the betrayal of the institution of marriage that sucker punched me. Not in my worst nightmares would I have thought that I would be simultaneously the victim of adultery, a widow, and a cancer survivor.

I couldn't sleep that night. I didn't drift off until after 3 a.m. I awoke at 7:30 a.m. and watched a new religious show. The message was entitled, "When Will This All Get Better?" The speaker said, "God doesn't have a calendar, but you can speed things along most times by just saying, 'Your will be done.'"

Something in me felt different that day. I had a few revelations. The most important one was that my calendar meant nothing. I didn't have control over the resolutions or timelines I desired. Even more important was my realization of why I couldn't stand people anymore, including, at times, some of my family. It was because I allowed them to keep me from saying fully, Your will be done.

My husband and I had been the best and brightest of our families as far as being risk-takers, educated learners, and successful achievers. I never could have admitted that truth before, but it was the truth. However, in the wake of the tragedies that had hit my children and me, I had been looking for other people, even my family members, to do something they hadn't ever done and couldn't do, which was to tell me how to live my life. Or what used to be our lives.

My husband and I had never asked this circle of people for anything, and we also never needed any help from them. I didn't like how I had changed. I was at one of the lowest places in my life, being incapable of guiding my children and needing now to reach out to family and friends. I didn't like the feeling of weakness that accompanied asking anyone for help or admitting that I might need them. I still find myself feeling this way. But during this period in my life, I didn't have my husband, who was the one person I could depend upon.

On this morning, I finally understood that what had been so frustrating was that I had been looking for something that could never come: help from others. I didn't care anymore because I wasn't looking for incompetent people to give me competent advice. I was going to stop second-guessing my decisions about anything and listen to my gut from that day forward.

If the universe had taken away my partner in life, my best friend, my husband, my protector, and my love, then I would have to stand alone and take on all of the pain and trouble by myself. I was angry, resentful, sad, and hurt, and I was suffering from a broken, ravaged heart. No one could feel that but me. So I said, Fuck it, and fuck you all who have been telling me to get on with my life or that my husband would have left me anyway. I gave every one of them a big, fat Fuck you.

These people invaded my life, claiming to understand with a hundred percent accuracy the matters that were between my husband and me: matters that were elusive even to me. I didn't want to listen to any of them or talk to any of them anymore about the tragedies in my life. I wanted to cut them off because they filled up so much negativity in my life where positivity could have had space to grow. Because I had been so used to being in a partnership in all things because of the friendship that existed between my husband and me, I had sought ready replacements. My desperation to get a new partner brought me to a low point where I finally realized that most people didn't give a damn, had no fight or courage, and weren't worth shit.

So until these friends of Job had walked in my shoes and experienced one iota of what I had endured, they couldn't fucking talk to me or ask me anything. They couldn't tell me what to say to God or to myself.

Fuck it. I was alone. I would take it all on. Alone.

In that moment, I knew that I had to kill. It was the only solution for my survival. I was living under siege. Enemies had infiltrated my heart and my home. A conspiracy surrounded me and had begun closing in with the help of my man.

So I killed. I killed the good girl.

I killed the good girl who lived deep inside me: trusting and obedient, careful, and afraid of the world outside her grandmother's door. If I hadn't killed that girl, I would surely have died.

So I murdered her. I killed the good girl who hesitated to face her enemies. When life became my enemy, my most formidable one, it was either let life kill me or kill the part of me that couldn't survive. There was a time during this decade-long ordeal when I was more than willing to let life do the deed. In fact, I had prayed with all the strength I had left to God to let my life leave me during the night. But God wasn't having it. He hadn't given up on me, even when I had given up on myself.

I have believed in God all my life, but the darkest of days and the longest of trials and have brought me to a place where no one else could find me. When stress becomes overwhelming, I go into my place of solace. I visit there often. In this place, I know that God is in control, and I await the miracles I trust that He will bring. I say, Your will be done, even to the point of death. It's not when the trial is over that we find God. It's in the going through. Say "Amen," somebody!

20

All the Way Back

I really don't know how I survived all of this, but it must be in the DNA. I come from a strong lineage of people of Black, Hispanic, German, French, and Native American heritage. From my younger years, through becoming an adult woman, I have been surrounded by women who knew how to battle.

I know now that I have to look out for myself. After all, not much has changed in the world from the days the police used to check in on me for DWB (driving while Black). I was even assaulted in an Equinox gym on the North Shore.

It happened when I went to work out one Sunday morning. The gym was virtually empty until one guy entered. Some people have the look of a bully. From his stance to the disdain in his eyes, this guy has had the demeanor of a bully for as long as I have known him. I had never spoken to him, but we crossed circles. My husband thought that this man was a racist asshole. To his credit, he never approached us, which was a smart move on his part.

Though Equinox on Long Island has gyms the size of city blocks with as many machines, this man decided that he wanted to use the one machine I was using. He stood over me. I finished my set, stopped to catch my breath, and looked down for a second. He put his hand in my face and waved, motioning for my attention.

"Can I help you?" I said.

"I want next," he demanded.

I got up and moved to another machine. There were at least fifty assorted machines, bikes, treadmills, and weight stations on this floor, and maybe five people on the floor.

He came over to where I had moved and stood over me again. "I'm cutting in here," he said.

This time, that was not happening. "I'm not finished with my set," I said and continued to pull the handles.

"Yes, you are," he said as he took his arm and knocked me off the machine.

I started screaming for help, and a woman came to my aid. Having seen the entire incident, she came to my defense. The managers arrived, and the woman explained the situation as this guy yelled, "I want her thrown out of the gym!" At that point, he was joined by another man who chimed in, "Come to my neighborhood, and we'll teach you a lesson!"

Note to self: No cursing to yourself.

Fuck that. I cursed the shit out of them both!

I was rushed into a side room while the managers went after the two cowards who bolted.

I called the police. Three cars showed up. The attacker was identified. I was hysterical. "What happened?" asked the officer.

Through tears, I tried to explain. But in my state of mind, I was hysterical. The officer asked me, "Why are you yelling?"

"You can go," I said. "I don't need your help. I have five (family members) on the job." Those were the magic words. It started an entirely new conversation.

"We are here to help. You're safe now. Can we call your husband?" one officer asked. "Thank you, but I'm alone. Widowed. No one to call." I was going to depend on myself.

Throughout this tragedy, I needed to hear some words of wisdom. I needed to be able to lie my head in someone's lap. I longed for my mother's tough love, which didn't come in hugs but in action: my teachers who she had faced down, the principals she had challenged, the guidance counselor who said I should hope to go to a commercial high school and the ugly boy who bullied me every day. My mother took care of them all.

When the tsunami of tragedy hit me, I just wanted to call her and say, "Mom, can you come with me today? Someone has bothered me." I knew that she would be my champion, my defender.

There isn't a shadow of a doubt that my mother would have dropped all to come, armed with her fearless nature and the facial expression that said, "Don't even."

But my mother, while still with me at the time, wasn't with me. Most patients with dementia and Alzheimer's are expected to survive a decade. Not my mother. Even though she lost speech, sight, recognition, and mobility, she held on as the fighter she was for fourteen years.

On the day that my husband died, my neighbors saw numerous people coming to my home. One neighbor asked my sister, "So, your mom finally passed?"

She responded, "No, it's my sister's husband."

I visited my mother many times throughout the fourteen years of her illness. In those visits, I whispered in her ear, "Mom, let go. Take your rest." It was so hard for me to see such a strong woman like this battle disease. I felt that she wouldn't want to see herself like this either, but she baffled even the medical professionals with how she fought.

As I write this and look back at how some things unfolded, I feel in my heart a selfish explanation for her "holding on." If I had to bury my mom in the middle of the worst days of my life, I don't know what damage it might have done to my family and myself.

When I received the call on the morning of August 21, 2014, I didn't expect to hear the words being spoken to me. She had gone. Five years after the death of my husband, my mother let go.

Her funeral was somber, and I cried for her life and the many years we lost because of her illness. I felt weak and distraught. A friend later commented to me that, although she knew I was a spiritual person, she saw a different side of me that day. She said, "You stood tall and confident. You sang your heart out, praising God, and you firmly held your father's hand. You looked like you were all the way back." Maybe this was what my mother was waiting for—that I come all the way back. She sized me up and closed her eyes in peace.

21

Still in the Battle

"And You Will Know My name is the Lord."
Samuel L. Jackson | *Pulp Fiction*

The Lord is my strength and my salvation. Whom shall I fear?

Fear? I fear no man or woman. The injustices I have suffered this last decade of my life have not softened or quieted me.

Yes. I pray. Yes. I believe in the Almighty. But don't mistake my love of God with weakness or an inability to meet you more than halfway if you dare to come for me.

It is said that any human who genuinely believes

God to be on his side is unbeatable. I know that I have not made it this far and survived all that I have without the divine intervention of God. There is no way that I'm still walking, speaking, and thriving without the help of the Lord. Doubt me if you dare. Laugh at me for my dedication to the belief that 'this battle is not mine, but it is the Lord's."

To all who sought to bring me down, rallied in my sorrows, and thought that they had brought about my defeat... when you hear me reciting my Scripture, it is like the lion devouring his kill before battle. I'm locked, loaded, and filled with the Holy Ghost. So say something.

I dare you.

Since the day my husband died, I have been in a battle. The battle for life, for home, for finances, for insurance, for respect, and for security. I haven't had a day of rest, peace, or tranquility when I could exhale and say, "Life is good."

I'm looking at the start of year eight in the battle. The news is never good. Phone calls with my legal team and financial advisors end with negative forecasts and talk of losing the fight for property that is rightfully mine. I wake up to this life and end my day thinking about tomorrow's bad news. I fear the mail. A certified receipt brings me to panic. And every issue needs a director, overseer, or second eye. Despite paying for professional services, I'm it. So, I have to be alert and listening and ready to respond at a moment's notice. I have to be smart, trust no one, and make my own plans. I'm my own cheerleader. The U.S. military has nothing on me. I'm truly an army of one. The battle is exhausting and non-ending, with no backup.

But it happened one day. Can't remember why or how. I think it was a day I finally listened to the words my pastor had said. I have always prayed, and I have read *Daily Word* for decades. I have faith. I trust in God. I filled myself with inspirational teachings, listening to Pastor Joel Osteen in my car at the request of my brother. In fact, my brother said to me, "You need Joel on an IV into your arm."

A friend of mine recently asked me what the *Daily Word* was. She had heard me mention it before. Instead of explaining, I decided to show her. I pulled out a well-worn, folded piece of paper. Well, actually, two papers. Back when I was totally enthralled in the madness and didn't know if I would go insane trying to weather the storm of life, my brother wisely suggested that I write a prayer to God. I asked God for guidance and for help to bring me through. I always prayed for certain things to become clearer and resolved in my life and for my family. The prayer I now pulled out was dated 2007. It was more than ten years that I had it stored in my wallet.

Wrapped around the prayer was a page from my *Daily Word* book. I don't know, maybe I thought the prayer would be protected if wrapped in such inspirational words, words that reminded me of my grandmother and comforted me as well. My prayers were answered. Not all my issues, of course, but the weight on my shoulders got lighter and I remained sane. Thank you, God.

Here are excerpts of the *Daily Word* that I have entrusted my prayers since I was a child:

Thursday, September 1, 2016
Fearless Living

My faith allows me to live boldly and vibrantly.

Living boldly and vibrantly does not mean denying my fears. I acknowledge any feelings of fear or anxiousness, but I don't let those feelings govern me or eclipse my awareness of God's omnipresent good. Instead, I recognize that now is the time to deepen and demonstrate the magnitude of my faith.

Centered in Truth, I affirm that there is no worldly circumstance that can defeat the power of Spirit in me. I recognize that I have the strength and wisdom to meet any and all challenges in my life.

Shifting fear to faith, I will prevail. Whether it is a physical challenge, emotional struggle, or financial concern, trusting in God, I always know what to do, where to go, and what to say. With faith, I boldly and vibrantly live each day to its fullest.

When I am afraid, I put my trust in you.—Psalm 56:3

Monday, September 5, 2016
Inner Peace

With mind and heart centered, I'm at peace.

A turning wheel has obvious movement on the outer edges while the center appears to remain still. The same holds true for my life. Despite what happens in the outer realm, I remain steadfast when I stay centered on the spirit of God within.

I begin with a shift in my feelings and attitude. As I focus my attention on God-life within, I move into a deeper understanding of the Divine. I find my peace.

I know what it feels like to be uplifted and radiant, buoyant, and expanded. Capturing that feeling, I move into a deeper awareness of the fluid movement of love in my heart. Now, I flow into that feeling. By taking such small steps several times each day, I find myself poised in a kind of peace that happens readily and easily. Inner peace sustains me at all times.

Peace be with you.—Luke 24:36

The messages from the *Daily Word* are simple, inspiring, and even a bit eerie at times.

Most times, when I'm at a low, I will read a message of the day that appears to have been written just for me. My favorite messages are entitled: "Let Go, Let God," which encourages you to turn the problem or situation over to God: to release the tight hold you have on the problem or a solution. Holding tightly restricts your faith that God is working it out. The tighter that you hold on, the more you make it impossible for God to work. I have collected many of these copies of the *Daily Word* during the years to pull out and read when I'm in my darkest moments.

Many of my most favorite topics are about serenity, comfort, faith, and resurrection. In fact, the Bible verse that is cited at the end of each passage serves as a lead into chapters in the Bible that reinforce the *Daily Word*.

Every single day before my feet touch the ground, I continue to recite one of those verses I happened upon from the *Daily Word*: "Trust in the Lord with all your heart, do not rely on your own insight. In all your ways acknowledge Him, and He will make straight your path."

The *Daily Word* helps me feel that when all looks bleak and when there couldn't possibly be a victory or a solution for my situation, someone hears me and answers.

So I listened to those messages, and I was ready. The unexpected test came on a visit to my lawyer's office. The first visit resulted in an all-out anxiety attack from his dramatic attempts to convince me that I needed to hire him to save my real estate properties. During the second visit, I listened intently and signed documents as my lawyer told me that I was going to lose in the end., This action was just buying me time. On the third visit, again, he gave his speech of doom. But this time, I sat erect and looked him straight in the eye.

Mid-sentence into his this-is-something-you-can't-win speech, he asked, "Are you listening to me? There is something different about you. You look defiant, and even your body language is different."

I replied, "I don't know, but what I do know is I don't get into a fight to lose it. And in the end, if I didn't win, it's because I ran out of time, trusted the wrong people, chose the wrong attorneys, and didn't have a team fighting for me like their own lives depended on them winning. So if you aren't going to fight for me, then I have to move on to a firm that will."

On that note, he responded, "Let's give them some shit!"

Now, we were on the same page.

I have been always waiting. Always waiting for that phone call that will change my life. Will someone call and tell me I lost my home? I'm tired of having a phone call dictate my life. And I won't let it anymore!

We were not "The Jeffersons." They were an example of a couple who embraced and never betrayed each other. My life went from being like Mrs. Jefferson to being the subject of a sensationalized article in a local tabloid. The topic of the article was "Husband Leads Double Life."

No one can believe any of this: that my husband would be unfaithful. For him, it was "God and family first." For almost three decades, I knew I had the "good boy," and he was the soulmate to the "good girl." But betrayal killed them both.

I didn't have any warning like the one I have written. The revelation of my betrayal happened at the exact time when I had to start the fight in the middle of my chemo treatment. Imagine that! In fact, I was the reason the treatment center got Wi-Fi in the treatment room: because I would bring my laptop and get to work for the three hours I sat there with the "Red Devil," as they call the strongest, chemo-fighting chemical running through my veins.

When I look in the mirror now, I see a woman who is fighting for what she is owed. My legal battle is finally on its last leg, and the prospects of winning look bleak. The case continues. I see a woman who has the permanent physical scars of a fight for life. I see a woman who wakes up to face the day ready for battle because I must be prepared for any and all bullets.

I'm a woman who stares at the possibility of losing all that I have built in my lifetime. I'm looking at a woman who spent her prime years trying to stay alive physically, mentally, and financially.

I'm a woman who stands in faith and hope. It is all I have to hold on to. Friends have left me, lawyers have betrayed me, yet every day, I'm still in the battle.

Make God Laugh

Ten years after the betrayal, my life isn't a reflection of what it had been. I'm older. I'm tired. I feel battle-weary and worn.

My view through a pair of magic glasses would find a woman in pain and struggling to keep faith despite the injustices of rulings against me in the battle against an insurance giant for payment on my husband's life. Yes. I feel betrayed by the lawyers I trusted to win and by a legal system that seems to favor the big guys and crush the little people whenever they think they might have a loophole in their favor, not to compensate the injured party.

I have continued to nurture my children, who have faced so much: from the whispers about their family from "friends and family" to the upheaval of their world and household, as well as the necessity of having to watch their mother battle for life and home. But through it all, they have survived and even excelled.

You see, I was not the only target of those who conspired against me which includes those who knew about the betrayal and kept it secret instead of revealing it to me and those who came after me for more of a share of the financial pot they thought they deserved because they slept with my husband for a few nights. Yes, come after one and you're coming after all. In the spirit of the warriors that tutored me, I took on every battle.

Even through my battle for life, I weathered the storm. I never stopped. You see, the one thing I had going against me after my husband's demise was that I didn't know who the enemy was or how many foot soldiers they had in their garrison.

I couldn't have pleasant conversations with anyone because I might have been speaking to an accomplice in this betrayal. I wanted to ask my banker *Did you know? Why did you not call me when you saw the sums of money being taken out of my account?* I wanted to scream at our life insurance broker *Did you not think you had a duty to warn me?* Anyone who represented us both, I now viewed as an unsuspecting accomplice.

Imagine waking up one day and finding out you don't have a dollar to your name. Think about what it would feel like to know you jointly owned a house with a woman you didn't know because your husband bought it for her and now you own it, too. Partners? Really?

But then imagine the glee you would feel when one Saturday morning a banker calls you asking for your dead husband.

"May I speak to him?"

"Nope. Dead." I said with no emotion.

Then, hearing the next question, "Well, can I speak to (her?)"

"Who?" I asked and added deadpan, "Nope. Don't live here."

And think about being able to find a bit of laughter in hearing the desperate bank representative looking to speak to anyone to get the back mortgage payments paid and finally asking, "May I ask who I am speaking with?"

"Yes, of course," I replied. "The wife. I am Dr. Teresa Taylor Williams."

"Oh. Hello, Dr. Williams. My name is Mary, and I work for Bank of America. We would like to offer you the opportunity to save this house. We truly don't want to foreclose and..."

I cut her off in mid-sentence. Cool and venomous. "Miss," I said politely, "I don't mean to be rude, but let me tell you where I stand on this house. The earth could open and suck the house, furniture, trees, grass, fence, and cars parked in the driveway down into the dirt like quicksand and then cover it up like it never existed, and I couldn't give a shit."

"Whoa!" the bank representative replied. "I think there's more to this story than meets the eye."

"Yes, there is," I said.

And for almost one hour, over a recorded line, I told her my story. She reciprocated by telling me about her own story dealing with a betrayal. At the end of the conversation, she asked if she could pray for me and my children.

"Please," I replied.

After praying, she said, "Dr. Williams, rest assured, we will never bother you again."

Those kinds of encounters I felt were little taps on the shoulders from God telling me I'm not sleeping. I see you, the one that I have brought this far. During the past year, I have had more of these encounters, and I have had helpers come into my life to help me get through.

I don't know what the future will bring, but I do know that I will never give up the battle against the legal injustices that have victimized me and the battle to regain my financial footing. I intend to surpass the accomplishments that Mr. Magic and I had together. I continue to work and grow my business, and I'm cultivating the young lives of two fierce, educated, and determined young women and one brilliantly educated, exceptional young man who I'm proud to call my own.

It's a strange thing to have been watched and dissected and betrayed in the daylight by someone you don't know, others you knew, and a man you called yours. But my mother always said, "What is done in the dark will come out in the light." The darkness has lifted off my life, and I'm working diligently to reveal what was done when I was deep in the dark. Now, thank God, I can see.

There was a time when I still had my plan. I would

live until the legal battles were settled so that I could rest in peace, knowing that my children were protected before I took that cap-side-up bottle I always kept by my bed. One day, I cleaned out my bathroom drawer and flushed down the toilet five unopened bottles of OxyContin and an assortment of other medications.

I don't know what was special about that day. It was years after the mastectomy and the death of my husband. I didn't have the same desire to leave this earth. I had been in the battle for survival for years by then. As I looked at the bottles, I realized that going forward, I would never use them. My spiritual strength and the need to secure the future and see this battle to the end has further eliminated any suicidal thoughts.

Eight years later, I'm still fighting the same legal battles. I'm still here. I'm still here.

Make God laugh. Tell him you have a plan. I made God laugh. I'm still here.

The Top 20 Considerations for Every Woman Upon Losing a Spouse

1. GRIEVING PROCESS: The grieving process can be
challenging and may temporarily hinder the pursuit
of new relationships.

2. SOCIAL EXPECTATIONS: Societal expectations and
cultural norms may influence how a black woman is
perceived when seeking new relationships.

3. FINANCIAL CHALLENGES: Economic disparities
can impact a woman's ability to achieve financial
independence, affecting her overall well-being and
confidence.

4. SINGLE PARENTHOOD: If the woman has children,
being a single parent may present additional challenges in finding time for herself and forming new
relationships.

5. LIMITED SOCIAL CIRCLES: Limited access to diverse social circles or communities may impact
opportunities to meet new people.

6. CULTURAL STEREOTYPES: Stereotypes and biases
may affect how others perceive and interact with
black women in the dating scene.

7. WORKPLACE DISCRIMINATION: Discrimination
in the workplace may contribute to stress and affect
overall life satisfaction.

8. Mental Health Stigma: The stigma surrounding mental health in the black community may hinder seeking support for grief and other emotional challenges.

9. Access to Healthcare: Disparities in healthcare access may impact a woman's ability to address physical and mental health needs.

10. Educational Disparities: Educational inequalities may affect opportunities for personal and professional growth.

11. Intersectional Discrimination: Experiencing discrimination based on the intersection of race and gender may pose unique challenges.

12. Media Representation: Limited positive representation in media can influence self-perception and impact confidence in seeking new relationships.

13. Cultural Expectations: Cultural expectations within the black community may influence relationship dynamics and choices.

14. Religious Factors: Religious beliefs and practices may impact dating preferences and choices for a black woman.

15. Lack of Representation in Leadership
Roles: Limited representation in leadership roles
may impact career opportunities and financial independence.

16. Dating App Bias: Online dating platforms may
exhibit biases that affect a black woman's experience
in the digital dating world.

17. Microaggressions: Experiencing microaggressions in daily life may contribute to stress and impact
overall well-being.

18. Family Expectations: Expectations from extended family members may influence relationship
decisions and independence.

19. Legal System Disparities: Disparities in the
legal system may impact issues related to inheritance,
property rights, and legal matters.

20. Historical Trauma: Historical trauma and its
impact on the black community may affect mental
health and relationships.

About the Author

Dr. Teresa Taylor Williams is the CEO and founder of TTW Associates, Inc. This consultant firm provides academic support services, professional development for administrators and teachers, and parental support. Dr. Taylor Williams offers grief, family, adolescent, and academic counseling as a mental health clinician. In addition, Dr. Taylor Williams is a consultant to school districts throughout New York State.

Dr. Taylor Williams has held numerous positions in both private and public education. As a former teacher, remedial specialist, and administrator for the New York City Board of Education, Dr. Taylor Williams has worked to improve the learning opportunities for all students.

Dr. Taylor Williams is also used as a specialist on mental health issues for Good Morning America, GMA3, ABC-TV News, and CNN.

Dr. Taylor Williams is a professor of psychology for the City University of New York, State University of New York, and Long Island University systems. Dr. Taylor Williams is a published author who has written extensively on education issues affecting minority students and social-emotional learning and the impact on mental health for students of color.

The most recent publication is a multi-cultural textbook, *The Purpose of Understanding: A 21st Century Look into Psychology.*

Dr. Taylor Williams is also the owner and publisher of New York Trend, a woman-minority-owned newspaper founded in 1989, and newyorktrendnyc.com, distributed throughout New York, Nassau, and Suffolk counties.

Dr. Taylor Williams is a member of the New York Mental Health Counselors Association and American Counseling Association, is certified by New York State, and is a Board-Certified Human Services Provider.

To Contact Traitmarker Media—

www.traitmarkeremedia.com
traitmarker@gmail.com

To Contact
the Author Directly—

doctaylorwilliams@gmail.com

www.ingramcontent.com/pod-product-compliance
Lightning Source LLC
Chambersburg PA
CBHW012028110726
47995CB00006B/1174